THE FUN KNOWLEDGE ENCYCLOPEDIA

The Crazy Stories Behind the World's Most Interesting Facts

Trivia Bill's General Knowledge

BILL O'NEILL

DON'T FORGET YOUR FREE BOOKS

Contents

Introduction

Welcome to The Fun Knowledge Encyclopedia: The Crazy Stories Behind the World's Most Interesting Facts! This book will take you on a rollercoaster ride, from the ridiculous to the laughable, to the simply interesting and thought-provoking. In 1992, a crate with 28,000 rubber ducks fell off a ship. Whatever happened to those rubber ducks? We'll give you all the details!

Who set the world record for the most consecutive hours of staying awake, and how did they do it? What exactly is the Sourtoe Cocktail, and where did it originate? Discover facts about everything from pop culture to crazy stories of the common folk, to history, to science. You'll be the only one of your friends to know how much the average cost is to climb Mount Everest or what part of the gingerbread man is commonly eaten first.

Prepare to laugh, shrug, shake your head, and learn tons of new, intriguing information. Who says reading can't be fun?!

Remember Forever

Did you know that there is a rare condition called hyperthymesia that allows people to recall almost every single detail of their life? That's right… every conversation, every date, every interaction… ingrained in their memory forever. Right now, there are an estimated 12-60 people in the entire world who have this condition and are able to remember each day of their lives.

People with hyperthymesia can think back to any date and remember what they did that day, what the weather was like, and even what they ate. Many of these people can mentally visualize these events, as well. While some people might think it would be awesome to be able to remember every detail of their life, many who have hyperthymesia find that it interrupts their day-to-day activities and relationships with others.

This condition is depicted in the television show *Unforgettable*, which aired on CBS and A&E from 2011 through 2016. The series centers on a police detective who has hyperthymesia and uses it to help solve cases. Can you imagine remembering every single detail of your life—even the ones you want to forget?!

Rocky Rocks Philadelphia

Rocky is an iconic movie that has made an impact on millions of viewers all over the world. After all, who doesn't love a good underdog story?! The film also had an undeniable impact on residents of Philadelphia who were there to experience the filming of *Rocky*.

The Italian Market, Schuylkill River, and Benjamin Franklin Parkway are just some of the Philadelphia landmarks recognizable in the film. But the connection to locals was more than that. Many locals can be seen in the background, especially in the most famous scene of Rocky running through the city as part of his training.

The orange thrown at Rocky as he runs? That was the owner of one of the stalls in the Italian Market. Because Sylvester Stallone was virtually unknown and the scene was being shot with a single camera, people didn't know that a movie was even being filmed. The stall owner completely improvised. Another fun fact: Rocky's signature outfit—the leather coat and fedora—was even purchased from a Philadelphia thrift store.

King of Rock and... Flowers?

Flowers are a key aspect of Valentine's Day... and anniversaries... and rock icons' funerals? When people look back on Elvis's funeral, they often recall the massive amounts of flowers. But, would you believe that for FTD, one of the leading flower delivery services, the day of Elvis's funeral set the record for the day with the most flower deliveries?

FTD alone delivered 3,116 flower arrangements for the August 18, 1977 funeral.

This vs. That: Calorie Edition

Unhealthy foods can often be disguised as healthier foods, which is being proven true every day by fast food restaurants. You'd be surprised to see the nutritional information of some of these foods. Let's take a look.

- McDonald's chicken Caesar salad has 730 calories and 53 grams of fat, while the Double Big Mac only has 680 calories and 38 grams of fat.

- A steak and white cheddar panini on a sub roll from Panera sounds pretty harmless, right? Believe it or not, it clocks in at 940 calories and 1520 mg of sodium. That's around ½ of your daily recommended calories and ⅔ your daily recommended sodium intake... in one sandwich!

- Getting a 10-piece bag of chicken bites at KFC may seem like a much better choice than opting for some of the other foods, like fried chicken wings, mashed potatoes, and biscuits. But would you believe that those 10 pieces contain a whopping 1300 calories?! You could eat an entire watermelon for the same number of calories and less than one-tenth of the fat.

Presidential Similarities

All former presidents of the United States are bound together for life, but the similarities between two former presidents goes beyond what is normal. Have you ever heard about the Lincoln/Kennedy paradox?

For starters, both Lincoln and Kennedy had previously been boat captains and were also the second children in their family. Both presidents were elected in the year '60—Abraham Lincoln in 1860, and John F. Kennedy in 1960. They each had three children living with them in the White House and had one child pass away during their presidency.

But that's just the beginning. President Lincoln had a secretary with the last name Kennedy, while President Kennedy had a secretary with the last name Lincoln. Upon each of their deaths, they were succeeded by vice presidents with the last name Johnson (Andrew Johnson and Lyndon B. Johnson).

Both John Wilkes Booth and Lee Harvey Oswald, the presidents' assassins, have fifteen letters in their name. Booth shot President Lincoln in a theater and then fled to a warehouse, while Oswald shot President Kennedy from a warehouse, then fled to a theater. These similarities are a bit eerie, right?! It seems as though Lincoln and Kennedy were twins born a century apart.

Red Pen Rage

We've all been there… getting a school assignment or business project back from a superior with red pen all over it. It makes you feel bad, right?! Well, studies show that you're not alone. Red pen really does have a psychological impact on people, and it tends to bring about feelings of anxiety or disappointment.

A study done by sociologists at the University of Colorado found that corrections written in red ink were more likely than corrections written in other colors to be perceived as "shouting" or "disciplining". This is because red is a color known for evoking emotions. No wonder we all hate seeing the dreaded red pen!

If you're looking for a color to have the opposite impact, try out a pen with blue ink. These have been found to enhance motivation and boost creativity!

Unclaimed Baggage Center

If you ever find yourself in Scottsboro, Alabama, a small town in the northeast of the state, you might want to visit one of the world's most interesting stores: Unclaimed Baggage Center. It's just as it sounds. This place actually purchases unclaimed luggage from airlines and resells the items from these bags. At the store, the luggage arrives on tractor trailers and is then divided and sorted. They dry-clean the laundry, appraise the jewelry, and test and clear out electronic equipment, then put them out for sale.

That's right… you can buy items that belonged to someone who never claimed them at the airport. The store was started in 1970, when a man named Doyle Owens came up with the idea to buy a truckload of unclaimed baggage in Washington, D.C. He sold the contents of the luggage on card tables in a rented house until the business became big enough to open a storefront.

Over the years, Owens developed relationships with airlines, and the store, which now spans more than a city block, remains the only lost luggage store in the country. While most of the baggage comes from airlines, some also comes from trains, buses, and trucks. Unclaimed Baggage Center boasts that they put out 7,000 new items each day and wash or dry clean over 50,000 items each month.

People have found some crazy things at the store, ranging from a bag with fifty vacuum-packed frogs to a 40-carat emerald, to a 4,000-year-old Egyptian burial mask. Maybe the person whose belongings you're sifting through had just gone on a trek of Southeast Asia, or maybe they went on an African safari and brought back tons of awesome souvenirs they never claimed! It's definitely a one-of-a-kind concept.

Not S'mores Before

Graham crackers may be a popular snack food— especially when it comes to making s'mores around the campfire—but that wasn't the purpose the creator had in mind. In the 1800s, the food industry was becoming more industrialized, with breads and baked goods being mass-produced more often.

Sylvester Graham was a minister who believed that he could use this change to—believe it or not—help people abstain from sex. His graham cracker recipe, then known as graham bread, was created with the intention of curbing sexual desires and serving as a form of birth control. The idea, from what researchers can tell, was that it was so bland that it could cause teenagers to forsake sex just to keep from eating another piece.

Those delicious graham crackers we're used to eating? Those came years later. Weird, right?! You'll never see graham crackers the same way again!

Angle, Pop, Clear, Glide!

Doc Emrick isn't as well-known as some of the other announcers in hockey, but he is known for his colorful descriptions and unique play-by-plays that set him apart from the other announcers. For the 2014 Olympics USA vs. Canada game, a fan counted how many words Emrick used to describe the movement of the puck, and the final count was startling: 153!

Some of the verbs he used include curled, skipped,

nubbed, finessed, dished, swatted, threaded, whistled, squibbed, struck, muscled, collared, angles, blasted, backchecked, and outletted. He'd make a great human thesaurus, huh?!

You Wanna Go Out?

When most people think of popular dating sites, they think of pages and apps like Tinder, OKCupid, and Plenty of Fish. But would you believe that YouTube, the king of internet videos, was originally created to be a dating website?!

The original plan was to have interested singles post a video introducing themselves and explaining what they were looking for in a date or significant other. However, when five days passed without a single video being uploaded, the co-founders, Steve Chen, Chad Hurley, and Jawed Karim, decided to open up the site to any video. They knew they had unique technology that gave anyone and everyone the ability to upload videos, so they wanted to get it out there any way they could.

It worked out in their favor: they sold YouTube to Google for $1.6 billion and have an average of one billion visitors each month!

Breakfast of Champions

Alex Trebek may be getting older, but that doesn't mean he's watching his sugar intake or changing his diet to consist of healthier foods. The *Jeopardy* host has said in interviews that he has two main breakfast choices: Snickers bars and Diet Pepsi, and Milky Way bars and Diet Coke. Despite two heart attacks and almost twenty different surgeries on his body, Trebek has no plans to change up his old reliable breakfast.

An Alum to Remember

Before Ted Kaczynski made headlines as the Unabomber, a domestic terrorist who sent mail bombs, he attended Harvard University. Unfortunately, someone in the Harvard Alumni Association didn't get the memo that Kaczynski is a serial killer serving life in prison and probably shouldn't be noted as a famous alum.

The class of 1962 celebrated their 50th anniversary in 2012 with a publication updating everyone on each other's life. Ted Kaczynski sent in a nine-line entry, with his awards section reading, "Eight life sentences, issued by the United States District Court for the Eastern District of California, 1998." He also listed his 664-page book, "Technological Slavery", which includes his famous "Unabomber Manifesto", as a publication of his.

For his address, Kaczynski wrote, "No. 04475-046, US Penitentiary – Max, P.O. Box 8500, Florence, CO 8126-8500." A spokesperson for the alumni association confirmed that it was, in fact, Kaczynski who submitted the entry, as all submissions by alumni are included in the report.

Can You Smell It?

With all of the new technology in the world and some of the highest-paying fans around, the NFL (National Football League) is always up to date on the trends… with the exception of one old reliable. For years, the NFL has been using ammonium carbonate, better known as smelling salts, to help bring unconscious players back to consciousness.

The smelling salts work by stimulating a nerve that runs from the nose into the brain. Many football players have attested to the effectiveness of the smelling salts, with some even going so far as to sniffing them in the middle of games to help increase alertness. Who would've thought something so simple could help fuel a multi-billion-dollar operation?!

Old School, Indeed

Before the days of Princeton and Oxford, University of Bologna was *the* university to go to. Why? Because it's been around for over one-thousand years! The school was founded as a "stadium" for students in Northern Italy, and it is for this reason that Universita di Bologna, as locals call it, is considered the oldest college of the Western world.

In the 11th and 12th centuries, scholars from all over would come to study law and literature. The 14th century brought about concentrations like theology, astronomy, and medicine, while the 15th century introduced Hebrew and Greek studies. When the Industrial Revolution took place in the 18th century, University of Bologna started focusing more on technological and scientific topics.

Although it has been in existence since 1008, the school didn't take its modern form until the late 1800s and early 1900s. The university now serves over 50,000 students each year and offers programs ranging from History and Cultures to Veterinary Medical Sciences. Throughout their long existence, they have produced alumni ranging from popes to members of European Parliament, to winners of singing competition shows.

World's Weirdest Museums

The days of simple art and science museums are long gone. Increasing in popularity are weird museums—there's no other way to describe them.

Dog Collar Museum—Kent, England
Bigfoot Discovery Museum—Felton, CA, USA
Beijing Tap Water Museum—Beijing, China
Momofuko Ando Instant Ramen Museum—Ikeda-shi, Japan
Museum of Bad Art—Dedham, Massachusetts, USA
Avanos Hair Museum—Avanos, Turkey
The Hobo Museum—Britt, Iowa, USA
The Bread Museum—Ulm, Germany
Clown Hall of Fame and Research Center—Baraboo, Wisconsin, USA

A Very Springer Governor

Jerry Springer may be best known for his self-titled talk show, but before the days of flashing lights and video cameras, Springer had a career in politics. Believe it or not, he served as the 56th mayor of Cincinnati, and he even ran for governor of Ohio. What ruined his campaign?

A young Springer, then 38 years old, admitted to paying for a prostitute. What's worse is that he was caught because he paid her with a personal check. Springer only came forward upon the spreading of false information, with rumors swirling that there were three women in the room, his check bounced, and he was arrested as a result of his conduct.

Moral of the story? Never pay for a prostitute with a check… or maybe you should. You could always end up with a popular talk show and a net worth of over $40 million.

Someone Got Off Easy

In 2014, a British woman sued her divorce lawyers, claiming that they had not warned her that getting a divorce would end her marriage. The woman, a practicing Roman Catholic, argued that a separation would have been more appropriate, and her lawyers should have suggested that instead. As one can imagine, the case was quickly dismissed.

Curious Case of the Prime Minister

Howard Holt was serving as Prime Minister of Australia when he suddenly disappeared in December 1967. Holt had been the Prime Minister for just over a year and a half at the time of his disappearance. He was swimming at Cheviot Beach, and, due to the rough seas, is presumed to have drowned. Some have their own theories on the disappearance, but it has been deemed to be an accident. The body has never been recovered.

See, Spot, Smell

Dogs are not only a man's best friend, they're also far superior when it comes to smelling. Their sense of smell is estimated to be somewhere between 10,000 and 100,000 times better—or more acute— than ours. To put it into perspective, if you dilute one teaspoon of sugar in a million gallons of water, dogs would be able to detect it. While humans have about six million olfactory receptors in their noses, dogs have upwards of 300 million. It's no wonder dogs are often used to help sniff out drugs and explosives.

Drama King

No one likes a parking ticket, but one man has taken it to the next level. Eugene Mirman is known for voicing Gene Belcher on *Bob's Burgers*. After spending the day out and about in a small New Hampshire town, he came back to find a $15 parking ticket on his car. The reason? He had parked his car backwards.

Mirman's response cost a heck of a lot more than the parking ticket; he took out a full-page ad in the town's newspaper. The ad mocked the town's ordinances that, if you study their website, reveal that cars cannot be backed up to the curb. He signed the ad, "With Great Disappointment in You." That's one way to make a statement.

More Than A Few Movie Mistakes

Titanic may be one of the most popular movies of all time, but that doesn't mean it's free of errors. In fact, while watching the film, you can catch a myriad of mistakes that no one working on the film caught. For example, throughout the film, Rose's beauty mark changes sides.

How about the fact that if you watch the part where Rose frees Jack in slow-motion, you can see that she visibly hits his wrist?! In the same scene, Jack's suspenders disappear. In another scene, you can even see one of the videographer's cameras in the reflection of a door. Chances are that the type of camera being used on the film wasn't around in 1912.

Of course, there are a few not-as-noticeable mistakes. These include glass reappearing where the safety axe is being kept, fixed parts of the ship suddenly disappearing from one scene to another, and Jack's hair magically slicking itself back in the third-class dancing scene. You'll never look at the movie the same way again!

Photic Sneeze Reflex

Have you ever heard someone tell you to look up at a light bulb or sunlight when you feel like you have to sneeze but just can't? They're not just making it up! Sneezing upon seeing bright light is known as the "photic sneeze reflex". It's one of those things that scientists can't quite explain even though it's proven to be an actual occurrence.

Ice, Ice Baby

For those looking for a unique vacation, ice hotels are the latest trend sweeping the globe. Ice hotels are exactly what they sound like—hotels made of (or at least incorporating) ice. At the Hotel Kakslauttanen Igloo Village is in Saariselka, Finland, guests can opt for a glass or snow igloo. The hotel also features an ice sculpture gallery and offers sled rides.

Snow Village and Hotel de Glace are the most popular snow retreats in North America. Located in Montreal, guests of Snow Village can stay in ice suites or igloos, sip ice cocktails, and dine in an ice restaurant. Just outside of Quebec City, the Hotel de Glace is known for its snow art and tours that show how the snow buildings are made.

For a regal experience, The Snowcastle of Kemi in Kemi, Finland, is the place to go. It's known not as a hotel, but as a "snow castle full of intricate ice sculptures and unique rooms. Like many of the other ice-centered retreats, this one is rebuilt every year for prime ice retreat season, but the Snowcastle is different in that it is built with a different, unique design each year.

Other hotels centered around ice are the Eskimska Vas (Eskimo Village) in Slovenia, Snow Village in Finland, Kirkenes Snowhotel in Norway, and Icehotel in Sweden. While staying at an ice hotel is a once-in-a-lifetime experience, it doesn't come cheap. Rooms/igloos can range from $300 all the way up to several thousand dollars per night.

Come See the Babies

Incubators have been around since the late 1800s, originally just to warm babies, but then helping premature babies everywhere thrive. However, they haven't always been in the same atmosphere you normally see them in. Because incubators were too expensive for most hospitals to have, Dr. Martin Couney, an innovative specialist in this area, turned them into an exhibit for the first time in 1903.

That's right, people would come and pay a fee to watch the babies. One incubator exhibit was a permanent fixture for decades at Coney Island, and others were added at Luna Park and Dreamland.

While many were skeptical and Dr. Couney was hesitant to charge people money, it was something that attracted public interest, and it helped save the lives of over 6,000 babies.

An Affair to Remember

They say affairs are the easiest way to kill a marriage, but how long before past trysts no longer matter? Antonio, a former military officer in Naples, Italy, divorced his wife in 2011 after finding letters his wife had written to a lover he had never known about. The twist? The man was 99 years old, his wife was 96 years old, and they were married for 77 years.

Antonio's wife, Rosa, had corresponded with her lover over sixty years earlier, and Antonio found the letters in a drawer. The split of the couple put a strain on the family they had built over the years, including five children and twelve grandchildren. As of the time of their divorce, they became the oldest couple in the world to get divorced. The title had previously been held by a British couple who divorced at the age of 98.

Name the Baby

While America doesn't have any set guidelines as to what you can and cannot name your child, other countries have much stricter stipulations. Sweden has an official law called the Naming Law, put into effect in 1982, that limits what parents can name their child. It originally served the purpose of preventing non-royals from giving their children noble names, but it now keeps families from choosing first names that are offensive. Names that have been rejected include Ikea and Elvis.

Amongst the countries with the harshest guidelines is Denmark. The country has a list of 7,000 pre-approved names to prevent parents from giving their children weird names. If you want to name your baby a name that is not on the list, you must get special permission, both from the government and your local church. More than that, unique spellings of common names are usually rejected, and last names cannot be used as a first name.

Germany's rules are a bit different, focusing more on gender. You must be able to discern a child's gender based on their name, and they can't have a name that negatively impacts their well-being. The local area in which the parents live has an office that decides if names are approved or rejected. Names like Maximillian and Nemo have been approved for boys, while Matti was rejected, as the office claimed it wasn't a name that distinguished gender.

In America, most people may find weird that celebrities select baby names like Apple, River, Saint, Apollo, and Titan, but they have the right to. Several states *do* have laws in regard to baby names, such as California banning the use of accent marks on birth certificates and Massachusetts limiting the number of characters in a person's name. Who would've thought baby names could cause such problems?!

Zeitgeist

While Spiderman and Superman are two of the most popular superheroes that come to mind, there's another superhero with quite an interesting superpower. Zeitgeist, whose real name is Axel Cluney, vomits on his enemies. To be more accurate, he secretes corrosive acid that is said to be able to melt or eat through anything. That's something special, huh?

Not So Sanitary

Subway systems are a popular way of traveling throughout cities, but they're nowhere near clean and sanitary. As a matter of fact, in 2007 and 2008, biologists from the University of Colorado went to New York City to analyze air samples in subway platforms. The results were... well, let's just say you'll be scrambling to find another means of transportation from now on.

The scientists found that around 15% of the particulates in the air were made up of human skin. The majority of these skin cells were from feet and heads of riders, but 12% came from less-than-pleasant body areas, such as belly buttons, armpits, and buttocks. There was also a higher amount of fungus in the subway station, which the biologists attributed to rotting wood on the subway tracks.

Help for Hire

Nowadays, hiring people to do chores or run errands for you is the norm, and Japan has taken hired help to the next level. A business called Ikemeso Danshi was created for female workers to hire good-looking men to come wipe away their tears.

That's right, these women pay to have a stranger comfort them. The company, which is based in the Kanto region, targets women who are overworked and overstressed. The women place an order then watch a sad movie with the man they've hired in order to get the tears flowing. Once they start crying, the man gently wipes away their tears. The cost for this service starts at about 7,600 yen, or $66.

Lost in Translation

With all of the confusing spelling and pronunciations, people often say that English is one of the hardest languages to learn. More than that, we have tons of words and phrases that just can't be translated 100% accurately into other languages. Check out a few of them…

- Trade-off
- Serendipity
- Auto-tune
- Facepalm

- Insight
- Specific descriptions of sights and sounds, such as gleam, glisten, and rustle
- "Piece of cake."
- "Adding fuel to the fire."

Why must the English language be so confusing?!

Idiom Control

Idioms are, whether we realize it or not, a huge part of everyday life. A penny for your thoughts? Idiom. Ball is in your court? Idiom. Kill two birds with one stone? Yet another idiom. Just as there is no direct way of saying these phrases in other languages, when we try to translate idioms from other countries, the results can be quite amusing.

"Tomaten auf den Augen haben." This is a German idiom that means that you're just not seeing the objects that everyone else is seeing. However, when translated to English, it means, "You have tomatoes on your eyes."

"Att glida in på en räkmacka" is a popular Swedish phrase that refers to someone that didn't have to put in the work to get to where they are. Translated to English, it means, "To slide on a shrimp sandwich" or "To slide on a shrimp bag."

A popular French phrase goes, "Les carottes sont cuites!" This phrase means that the situation cannot be changed, but it translates to, "The carrots are cooked."

In Germany, "Die Katze im Sack kaufen" is a way of saying that you bought something without first inspecting or checking in. The English translation is, "To buy a cat in a sack," but the more commonly-used equivalent is "buying a pig in a poke."

There is a Portuguese idiom that goes, "Empurrar com a barriga." This translates to, "Push with the belly," but is used to refer to postponing something important that needs to be done.

Penis Protection

Thimphu is the largest city in the small country of Bhutan, located in the Himalayas. Residents of the city also have a unique fixation on one item in particular—the phallus. Erect penises are painted in artwork, and statues are displayed on rooftops and in cities. The Buddhists in this kingdom believe that having phallic artwork and devotion will protect from evil and aid in fertility. Now, this puts a whole new meaning on using protection.

Just Searching for the Loo

An elder from the Adnyamathanha, an indigenous Australian tribe, was exploring gorges in the area. As luck would have it, the man, Clifford Coulthard, has to use the bathroom, so he searched for an empty space to "do his business." The area he came across was more than just a prime location for going to the bathroom in private, it was proof of the earliest human settlement in Australia.

The site, known as Warratyi, offers proof that there were settlers in the area 49,000 years ago, which is 10,000 years earlier than scientists had previously thought. The rock shelter had a blackened roof, which tipped Coulthard off to its significance. Scientists have since been able to recover over 4,000 artifacts and 200 bone fragments. Not too shabby for a bathroom trip, huh?

Richer Than They Seem

Casinos are a popular form of entertainment in the United States, but Indian casinos aren't just for the visitors. As a matter of fact, they're also helping make some tribes extremely wealthy. The Shakopee Mdewakanton tribe, located outside of Minneapolis, Minnesota, is the richest tribe in America. They own two casinos that allow for a 99.2% unemployment rate amongst the 480 members of the tribe. How?

The revenues have reached an estimated $1 billion per year, which works out to about $84,000 per month, per person. These men and women are living in huge mansions, vacationing on yachts, and driving the newest, fanciest cars. That's a far cry from the picture of Indian tribes most people have in their mind!

Dog Days Are Over

In October of 1988, a dog fell to his death from a 13th story balcony in Buenos Aires. As if this wasn't heartbreaking enough, the story gets more peculiar, as the dog's death triggered the death of three others. The dog, named Cachi, knocked a 75-year-old woman in the head, which caused her to die instantly. Another woman, Edith Sola, was hit by a bus while watching the scene from the middle of the street. Finally, a gentleman who witnessed both incidents had a heart attack and died on his way to the hospital.

Mona Lisa Twinning

No portrait is as famous as the Mona Lisa… except maybe an earlier version of the Mona Lisa. The earlier version is known as the Isleworth Mona Lisa, and it was discovered by a British art collector shortly before World War I. The painting was sent to America during World War I, then made its way back to Italy before finally being sent to a Swiss bank vault, where it remained for forty years until 2012.

Art historians and experts have been working to determine whether or not the portrait is authentic, but it is believed that the elements are similar enough to deduce that the Isleworth Mona Lisa was, in fact, also painted by Leonardo da Vinci. Others believe that this other painting is just a centuries-old reproduction of the original Mona Lisa, much like people can turn to the internet for reprints in today's times. Either way, it is a find that has art enthusiasts questioning five hundred years of art knowledge.

Pilot's Choice

Airplane food has garnered a reputation for being less than stellar, especially in economy class, but that's just a part of flying, right? Not if you're the pilot. Pilots often get a business or first-class meal, or sometimes an entirely different menu made specifically for the pilots. Those soggy green beans you're forced to suffer through? The chicken that doesn't quite look like chicken? Don't expect your pilot to be eating those anytime soon.

In another interesting twist, there are several airlines that require the pilot and co-pilot to eat different meals. The reasoning is simple. If, for whatever reason, a meal causes food poisoning, one of the pilots will still be well enough to fly the plane.

Saved by The Music

Joseph Haydn is an icon in classical music, and it was no different during his lifetime in the late 1700s and early 1800s. In fact, his music saved lives. On February 2, 1795, Haydn, a local celebrity, directed a highly-anticipated new symphony at the King's Theatre in London. The audience moved forward to try to get as close to this icon as possible, emptying the middle area of the theater. In a twist of fate, a chandelier crashed down from the ceiling, hitting the seats the spectators had recently vacated. A passion for music—literally—saved their lives.

A Curse is a Curse

Pele is known as the volcano goddess of Hawaii, and it seems that tourists take her wrath very seriously. Thousands of people visit the Hawaii Volcanoes National Park each year, and quite a few of them take sand, shells, and rocks as a memento from their trip. What these tourists didn't suspect is what bad fortune would come as a result taking these items.

One such man is Timothy Murray, a man who saw his luck change after visiting Hawaii Volcanoes National Park in 1997. Murray, amazed at the beauty of the park, scooped some black sand in a bottle to take home. When he returned home, his life fell apart. His pet died, his engagement fell apart, and he was arrested in connection to a computer copyright infringement case. Murray mailed the sand back to the local post office in Hawaii, believing it would reverse his luck.

Apparently, Timothy Murray is not the only one who blames Pele for their problems. Tourists send mail addressed to "Queen Pele" every day, hoping that returning what they "took" from her will reverse their misfortune. Whether or not there's any correlation between a visit to Hawaii Volcanoes National Park and newfound bad luck is a matter of opinion. Moral of the story? Don't upset Pele.

Golden Girls Gone Tough

Bea Arthur might be known as sassy Dorothy on the popular show, *The Golden Girls*, but the actress's impressive résumé goes far beyond her acting credits. Arthur, who died in 2009, served in the military for two and a half years when she was 21 years old. She always denied her time in the military, but documents reveal that she did serve. As a matter of fact, she met her husband, Private Robert Arthur, while she was enlisted. Bea served as a truck driver and typist, ending as a staff sergeant when she was honorably discharged in 1945.

A Titanic Secret

Bertha Mayne lived an average life as a singer in Paris, but she held onto one secret, her experience aboard the *RMS Titanic*. In 1911, she had met a young hockey player, Quigg Baxter, and they fell in love. Wanting to accompany him back to Montreal, she joined him aboard the world-class *Titanic*. She was 25 years old at the time.

In order to keep things proper and avoid any suspicion, Baxter got Mayne a first-class stateroom under the name "Mme. De Villiers". The night of the sinking, he persuaded Bertha to get in lifeboat 6, along with his mother and sister. The three of them survived while Quigg Baxter presumably drowned. After the tragedy, she spent several months with the Baxter family before returning to her life and career in Paris.

Bertha never shared her experience with anyone until she was much older. She told her nephew she had been aboard the *Titanic* with a rich Canadian man, but no one believed her story. It wasn't until after her death that her family found photographs and letters to support her story.

McEnroe Can't Score

John McEnroe has made his name as one of the greatest tennis players in recent history, but, unfortunately, he has also made another list: the list of lowest-rated television shows. In 2004, McEnroe launched his talk show, simply called *McEnroe*, on CNBC. The first week of the show raked in a measly 174,000 viewers, and it declined to reach under 40,000 viewers on at least one occasion. This earned the show a 0.0 rating by Nielsen Media Research. Needless to say, the talk show was canceled after just 22 episodes.

The Last Supper

Prisoners' last meals have become a topic of conversation and public interest, to the point where many states and prisons have websites or webpages dedicated to listing the contents of each condemned prisoner's last meal. In 1995, Thomas Grasso made it his final mission to share his final meal mishap with the world.

Grasso, a convicted murderer, was on death row

awaiting his execution. For his last meal, he requested steamed mussels, a double cheeseburger from Burger King, half of a pumpkin pie, a strawberry milkshake, and Spaghetti-O's. Other variations say that he also requested a second strawberry milkshake, a lemon cut into wedges, and steamed clams.

Grasso's focus was on one single part of his meal. His final statement to the media was, "I did not get my Spaghetti-O's. I got spaghetti. I want the press to know this." Talk about a rough ending.

The Gingerbread Connection

Gingerbread men can bring about much more than just holiday cheer. Dunkin' Donuts decided to take it to the next level and survey customers about their gingerbread cookie-eating habits. They asked over 5000 people and found that 64% of them eat the head of the gingerbread man first. A neurological researcher says that this means that those people are more headstrong. 20% start with the legs, which indicates that those people are more sensitive. Finally, 16% go for the arm first. What does that say about them? Well, it depends which arm. Biting the right hand means that the person is generally pessimistic, while the left arm indicates creativity.

What Side Is He On Anyway?

Juan Pujol went by the codename GARBO during World War II. Born in Barcelona, he fought in the

Spanish Civil War, claiming to have fought on both sides. He decided to use his deception skills to serve the role of a British double agent in the Second World War. Pujol was able to convince Germany that he was on their side and over the course of several years deliberately fed them false information.

GARBO created an entire fictional network of agents and was given information about defense tactics by the unknowing Germans. They told him that they believed that the Allies were preparing to invade Europe, and they tasked him with keeping them informed and up to date on any development. Meanwhile, Pujol's responses were all a part of a plan to distract them and help the British carry out Operation FORTITUDE.

The cherry on top of this twisted situation? Pujol received decorations from both Germany and England. He was awarded an Iron Cross by Germany and an MBE (Member of the Order of the British Empire) by Britain. He is considered one of the most effective double-agents of all time.

Jacuzzi Doozy

Ask anyone what comes to mind when they hear the word "jacuzzi and they'll all say the same thing. It's a luxury tub, a hot tub, or a jetted tub. But jacuzzi is one of those words that is often misused. Jacuzzi is actually the name of the most popular portable spa manufacturer. It's like Post-It notes, Q-tips, or a

Xerox machine, in that the brand name has since become a commonly-accepted name for the entire group of products. What most people think of as a jacuzzi is actually just a spa… unless, of course, it is actually made by the Jacuzzi brand.

Old, Old, and Older

Sylvester Magee's headstone says that he was born on May 29, 1841, in North Carolina, and died on October 21, 1971, in Mississippi. That's right… that would make him 130 years old at the time of his death. Magee's obituary also claimed that he was the "last American slave." According to stories he told, he was sold at Enterprise, Mississippi, and served as a gravedigger throughout the Vicksburg siege.

On his 124th birthday, Sylvester Magee was sent a congratulatory letter from President Lyndon B. Johnson, and he was named by President Nixon as the oldest citizen in the United States in the 1960s. To this day, it remains a mystery as to whether or not Magee was, in fact, born in the 1840s and raised as a slave, or if parts of his story are just that—a story.

Bus-ted

Crazy news stories aren't new in this century. In 1947, William Cimillo was a bus driver for Surface Transportation Company, for whom he had worked for 17 years. Instead of driving his usual route, he one day decided to head for New Jersey. For days, no one heard a thing from him. His family was worried, and there were rumors that his bus had been hijacked or that he had been in a horrible accident.

Surface Transportation Company received a telegram from Florida two weeks after Cimillo went missing, requesting $50. He had run out of money. It was later found out that Cimillo had spent those two weeks driving down the East Coast of the United States, and he claimed that he just needed a break from the city and his life. Police and a mechanic were sent to escort him—and the bus—back to New York City. While this crime would get you years behind bars in today's society, Cimillo's story had a much different ending.

His fellow bus drivers helped pay for his defense and ultimately aided in getting the charges dropped. People were intrigued by the bus driver's adventure, which led the Surface Transportation Company to offer Cimillo the option to continue his work. He drove the bus for sixteen more years.

False Advertising

Constructed from bricks and stone, the Winecoff Hotel was known as one of the fanciest, most glamorous hotels in the Southeastern United States. The hotel was built in 1913, and it was touted as being "fireproof". As such, there was no sprinkler system or fire escape plan in motion. Unfortunately, this resulted in the death of 120 people. On

December 7, 1946, a fire broke out in the hotel, and people died from the fire and from jumping trying to escape the blaze. Much like the *Titanic* claiming to be "unsinkable", the Winecoff's reputation for being "fireproof" was false.

Another Mother's Day?

Anna Jarvis founded Mother's Day in the early 1900s, starting as what she called a Mother's Friendship Day to try to form unity between Confederate and Union mothers. This fueled her mission to create a day that would honor mothers all over the country. It started as a Mother's Day church service and became widely publicized and also highly criticized by members of the senate.

Nowadays, Mother's Day is celebrated by most everyone across the country. However, if it were up to Anna Jarvis, that would not be the case. Just fifteen years after starting the movement of celebrating mothers, Jarvis began telling people to stop celebrating Mother's Day. She felt that it had become too much of a commercial holiday and had lost its meaning.

Jarvis applied for a trademark for the words "Mother's Day", but she was denied. FTD, a leading flower company, offered to give her a percentage of sales of carnations for Mother's Day, but this made her angrier at the commercialization of the holiday. She even fought against charities that included

Mother's Day in their fundraiser marketing and protested the sale of carnations. One of Jarvis's last public appearances was petitioning for the abolition of Mother's Day.

Taking Phony to the Max

Everyone knows that cell phone contracts can get out of hand. There are contract fees, internet fees, upgrade fees, and even fees to end a contract. One Chicago man took his efforts to get out of his contract to an extreme level. After learning that he would have to pay $175 to get out of his Verizon Wireless contract, Corey Taylor faked his own death. He created a fake death certificate and had a close friend fax it. Unfortunately for him, Verizon eventually caught on, but he still feels that his extreme efforts sent a message to phone companies about how much customers hate the hidden fees in contracts.

Another Verizon customer took on another tactic: finding a loophole. After being told she would have to pay $150 to end her contract, Sandy Loehman read all of the fine print of her bill, looking for a way out. She found what she was searching for when she read that the price for receiving text messages from an international source had gone up by five cents. Generally, phone companies will cancel phone contracts if a change in charges has a negative impact on the customer, so Loehman argued with five different Verizon representatives until they agreed to waive the cancellation fee.

Party of One

Monowi, Nebraska, is known as the smallest incorporated town in the United States. The closest hotel is thirty minutes away, and the last big event at the town church was 50 years ago. One more thing: the population of Monowi is one. Elsie Eiler is 83 years old, and she is also the sole resident of Monowi. The village previously had a population of two, until Elsie's husband Rudy died in 2004.

Despite its small population, the town has a bar and tavern and a library, both managed by Elsie. In the 1930s, Monowi was home to 150 people, including Elsie and her family. The rest of the town moved on, while Elsie stayed, saying simply that she loves living there and has lots of friends in surrounding towns. Tourists visit regularly to meet Elsie and see this forgotten town.

Get Your Hot Dogs

Hot dog carts are a staple of every New York City street, but most would be shocked at the outrageous price tag. Mohammad Mastafa, a vendor in New York, has said that he pays the parks department $289,500 a year just to operate one cart near the Central Park Zoo. In less popular areas, fees are lower, with an estimate of $14,000 for Astoria Park and $1,100 in Pelham Bay Park in the Bronx. Cart owners must bid on their spots to secure them for use.

Cart revenue ranges vary greatly not only from cart to cart, but from day to day. Mohammad Mastafa's employee says that their cart makes around $750 each week in the summer. Other coveted areas around Central Park run around $200,000 a year. That's right… the fee to operate a single hot dog cart for one year is enough to pay over three years of rent for a two-bedroom apartment in the heart of New York City.

Love Bite

If you get bitten by mosquitos a lot, it might be more than just chance. Studies have been done to see what mosquitos are attracted to, and it turns out that mosquitos bite people with Type O blood almost twice as much as they bite people with Type A and B blood. Exercise plays a factor, too. Those who exercise more often generally have a higher buildup of lactic acid and heat in their body, which attracts insects.

Another factor, believe it or not, is suggested to be beer intake. A study has found that insects are more likely to be attracted to you after drinking a bottle of beer, but scientists aren't quite sure why. If you're pregnant, watch out… mosquitos are twice as likely to bite a woman if she's pregnant. If you have O blood, work out a lot, and drink beer or are pregnant, make sure to bring the bug spray next time you're outside.

Flying with Kitty

EVA offers a truly one-of-a-kind flight experience in the company of a beloved icon: Hello Kitty. The airline has a partnership with the Hello Kitty brand, as well as numerous planes that are Hello Kitty-themed. The flight experience begins with a pink gate at the airport centered around the character, including a gift shop that puts all other airport gift shops to shame.

Depending what flight passengers are on, the seats are made up with Hello Kitty pillows, blankets, and even a barf bag. Snacks are served in packaging with Hello Kitty designs, and the bathroom is filled with Hello Kitty-printed toilet paper. Before landing, guests can choose to purchase items from a catalog, ranging from a Hello Kitty model airplane to a Hello Kitty apron.

Going Out with A Bang

It's not out of the ordinary for clowns to show up at birthday celebrations or holiday festivities. But, thanks to a company in Ireland, they'll now be able to appear at funerals. The company, called Dead Happy Ireland, has one simple mission: to make funerals a happier occasion. Gerry Perry founded the company after hearing his friends talk about how they'd like their funeral to be more of a celebration than a downer.

As part of their service, clowns will appear at funeral homes, graveside services, or at a wake in one's home. If customers decide to use a clown for two or more of these events, they receive a discount. An advertisement they posted claimed that they'll make balloon animals, bring squirt guns, and even jump into the grave, based on the mourners' preferences. That's one way to make an exit.

A Winning Cocktail

Breaking a world record is no easy feat. Just ask the team at Porco Lounge in Cleveland, Ohio. On November 11, 2016, employees at the bar crafted what became the world's largest daiquiri. The daquiri weighed in at 95 gallons and was the idea of two bartenders, Dan Watson and Jordan Anderson. They used a 100-gallon barrel that Dan's wife decorated to look like a tiki mug and took 38 minutes to prepare the drink.

The First Mother

John F. Kennedy's mother, Rose Kennedy, had a project where she used to collect signatures of prestigious and noteworthy people to give out as gifts. Some of the autographs she obtained included Robert Frost, David Ben-Gurion, and President Dwight D. Eisenhower. In 1962, Rose even went so far as to request a signature from Soviet Union Premier Nikita Khrushchev shortly before the peak of the Cuban Missile Crisis.

Once she obtained the signed photograph, which was of Khrushchev, President Kennedy, and First Lady Jackie Kennedy, she requested that her son sign the photo, as well. This prompted President Kennedy to write a letter to his mother, requesting that she ask permission before requesting autographs from any future world leaders.

Covering All Their Bases

Match.com and Tinder are two of the most popular resources in online dating nowadays. Princeton Review is a premier tutoring and test preparation center. What do they all have in common? They were both previously owned by the same parent company, Match Group. When asked about why they would opt to get involved in both dating services and educational services, the group explained that there are quite a few similarities and core competencies between the two.

A statement released about the acquisition in Fall of 2015 detailed how Match.com, Tinder, and Princeton Review are all centered on strong user interface development, paid customer acquisition, and free basic features combined with paid premium features. The company organized their business into two categories: "dating" and "non-dating".

Always States the Same

A survey done by the United States Census Bureau has shown that 59% of Americans reside in the state in which they were born. This varies by state, with 78.8% of people in Louisiana, 76.6% of people in Michigan and 74% of people in Pennsylvania staying in their home state. On the opposite end, under 40% of people born in Alaska, Nevada, and Arizona live there for most of their lives. The most common moves from state to state in 2010 included California to Texas, New York to Florida, Florida to Georgia, and California to Arizona.

A Dictionary by Any Other Name

The Oxford English Dictionary is one of the most popular dictionaries in the world, but the initial plans took a lot longer than anticipated. It was decided by members of the Philological Society of London that the existing dictionaries were not complete enough, and an agreement was made with the Oxford University Press in 1879 to begin work on what is now known as the Oxford English Dictionary.

The plan was to create a 6,400-page compilation of all vocabulary, with a projected timeframe of ten years. James A.H. Murray, who led the project, realized it would take much longer than planned when, after five years of work with his colleagues, they had only gotten up to the word "ant". It took over forty years to complete the dictionary, with Murray overseeing an entire team on the project.

Unfortunately, Murray didn't live to see the final result of his work. He died in 1915, over thirty years after he first started working on the project. The first version of the Oxford English Dictionary was released in April 1928, with over 400,000 words spanning over ten volumes. After its release, work immediately began on the next edition.

From Dealer to Actor

Tim Allen may be a world-famous actor and comedian, but, before the days of *Toy Story* and *Last Man Standing*, he was living a very different life. Back in 1978, at the Kalamazoo/Battle Creek International Airport, Allen was caught with 1.5 pounds of cocaine on him. He was charged with drug trafficking and was looking at a life sentence. Lucky for Tim Allen, turning over the names of over a dozen other drug dealers shortened his sentence to three to seven years. He got out of prison in just two years and four months and continued on with his comedy career.

Driving in Spain

Spain has some pretty peculiar rules when it comes to driving. Check them out!

- It's illegal to drive while wearing flip flops, or while being shirtless or barefoot.

- If you park on sand that is deemed "protected", you could receive a fine up to 6,000 euros, or $6,665.

- If a driver is caught kissing a passenger or biting their nails, they can receive a fine.

- The driver's ears must be visible at all time.

- Having the radio on while filling your car's gas tank can result in a fine.

- Driving with a hand or arm out the window can cost you a 100 euro ($110) fine.

Here's the Point

Growing up, many of us were taught that it's rude to point at someone. But why? It turns out, if you look back to hundreds of years ago, pointing was used as a way of casting a spell on someone or signal an evil eye. A quote from the Moor of Venice goes, "A fixed figure for the time of scorn, to point her slow unmoving at her."

Couldn't Bear It

Adelia Trujillo was an independent woman living in Mora, New Mexico, in 2001. Despite being 93 years old, she walked without a cane, and she still had the spunk she was known for. For obvious reasons, her family figured that, should anything happen to her, it would likely be a result of her old age. In a cruel twist of fate, Trujillo died on August 18, 2001. How? A 250-pound bear broke into her house and killed her. This was the first death by a bear in New Mexico in at least a century. It is estimated that about 45 people were killed by black bears in North America over the course of the last century, making it an average of less than one person per year.

That's Some Strange Living

Strange houses are pretty common these days. Take the Leaf House in Brazil, for example. It was made without hallways and the intent to look like a giant flower. The Everingham Rotating House in Taree, Australia, is shaped like an octagon and rotates 360°. Pretty impressive, huh?

That's just the tip of the iceberg. There's a house called the Steel House in Lubbock, Texas. The architect behind the building treated it more like a piece of artwork or a sculpture, changing the design as he went along. The Sliding House in Suffolk, England, looks like your ordinary farmhouse from the outside, but there's one major difference. In a matter of minutes, the outer shell can be completely removed to reveal a glass inner shell.

The Crooked House of Windsor is the oldest house of the bunch, dating back to 1592. As its name suggests, it is built on a slant. Not only that, but it also formerly had a secret passageway to Windsor Castle. In a world of tiny houses and manufactured homes, nothing should come as a surprise at this point.

Are They Really Twins?

Amy Elliot was born in Waterford, Ireland, on June 1, 2012, four months premature. She weighed just over one pound, and she spent a great deal of time in an incubator until she was strong enough to survive on her own. In the meantime, Amy's twin-to-be, Katie, remained in the womb. The twins' parents decided that, after hours of labor, they would let nature take its course.

Doctors say that surviving as a twin born at 23 weeks is incredible enough, but the story doesn't end there. After three difficult and stressful months, Katie Elliot was born. The Elliot twins were born 87 days apart, setting the world record for longest amount of time between the birth of twins. The previous record was set in 1995 and 1996, when twins in Pennsylvania were born 84 days apart.

Can You Hear Me Now?

Paul Marcarelli became a recognizable face when, as the spokesperson for Verizon, he could be seen in commercials talking on his cell phone, asking, "Can you hear me now?". Marcarelli averaged $6,000 per commercial and was bound by the contract not to speak about his job or take any other acting jobs. The job lasted twelve years, but he wasn't sad to see it come to an end. At his grandmother's funeral, a friend of the family whispered Marcarelli's signature phrase. Neighborhood kids used to drive by his house in the middle of the night and yell, "Can you hear me now?"

Not Always Nine Innings

The baseball we watch on television or at the stadiums may be a standard nine innings (except, of course, in the event of extra innings), but this wasn't always the case. Before 1856, the game was played until the scores of the two teams equaled 21. The idea of limiting the number of innings didn't come about until a tied game resulted in sixteen innings.

Originally, members of the New York Knickerbockers, who set the standards and rules, wanted to have seven players on the field and seven innings. This idea was vetoed, and it was decided that the game of baseball would have nine innings and nine players on the field, just as we have today.

Stuck During Sex

Penis captivus may sound like some sort of made-up X-rated wizard spell, but it is actually the name for an existing occurrence. Penis captivus is when a man's penis gets physically stuck in a woman's vagina. The cause is unknown, but it is suspected that it has to do with a woman's vaginal muscles contracting during orgasm. This is rare and generally only happens for a matter of seconds, but it's still enough to scare some away from sex for a while.

History of Cotton Candy

Cotton candy is a carnival, sports game, and circus favorite. But where did it originate? The first cotton candy was introduced by two men in Tennessee in 1897. At the time, they called it "fairy floss", and it cost half as much as admission to fairs at that time. Machines, however, were unreliable, and it was hard to keep up with the demand of this popular fair food. The modern spring-base machine was invented by Gold Medal Products in 1949. To this day, they are one of the sole manufacturers of cotton candy machine.

How is the cotton candy made? Sugar is the sole ingredient. It is melted to liquid form, then it is spun through holes that cool the sugar while also melding it into its signature shape. The coloring, as you might have guessed, comes from food coloring. If you're crazy for cotton candy, join in and celebrate National Cotton Candy Day on November 7th of each year!

A Very Beatles World

The Beatles had an impact on much more than just the music scene. They weren't afraid to make their political opinions known, which fans took notice of. While many people know that The Beatles took a stance against the Vietnam War, not as many people know that they also took notice of the segregation in the southern United States.

That's right, the band refused to play at a concert in Jacksonville, Florida, after finding out that it would be segregated. It became a part of their contract that they would not pöay for segregated audiences, as The Beatles' home country of England had much better race relations than that of the United States. The members of the band commented that they hadn't realized how bad the racial issues were in the United States until they broke through and traveled to America.

Do You Care About Carrots?

Baby carrots are a key part of many school lunches, vegetable trays, and healthy snacks. However, unlike regular carrots, these miniature carrots aren't grown naturally and sold the same way. Baby carrots are full-sized carrots cut into smaller sections, peeled, and pumped through pipes, then formed into the little carrot pieces that are now recognizable on store shelves everywhere.

The process begins when carrots are brought by truck to a processing plant. They are put in ice water until their temperature is brought down enough to prevent spoiling. At this point, they are divided into groups by thickness, as carrots that are too thick will be sold as whole carrots or used to feed cattle. An inspector must sort through the carrots to make sure there are no rocks or bad carrots that passed through.

Automatic cutters chop these carrots into two-inch pieces, then these pieces go through pipes to the peeling tanks. They go through two peeling processes: the rough peel and the final peel. Finally, the carrots are bagged by a machine and kept in a refrigerator or cold storage container until they are ready to be shipped out.

This system has been in use for around thirty years. It originated when Mike Yurosek, a packing plant manager, decided that there must be a better option for the 400 tons of "bad" carrots he threw away each day. He started off by using a potato peeler and knife to peel and cut the full carrots. An industrial green bean cutter was used to cut them into smaller pieces, which is how the two-inch size came about. Yurosek sent them to local grocery stores to test out, and they were a hit.

Skin Cells Everywhere

It is estimated that the average human body has 1.6 trillion skin cells. Obviously, this can vary by size, but it still averages about 16% of your entire body's cells. Whether you realize it or not, you're losing skin cells every day. A whopping 30 or 40 thousand skin cells fall off every hour. That means, each day, you're losing nearly a million skin cells.

Skin cells go everywhere. They become dust and debris. The average person sheds over 8 pounds of dead skin each year. These dead skin cells are called the stratum corneum, and they fall off to make room for a new layer of cells that are growing underneath. It's a process that no one notices or feels, but it's happening every minute of every day.

Drunk Doggies

One of Queen Elizabeth's footmen had a popular party prank that got him into some deep trouble. Matthew King was known for putting alcohol into the queen's corgis' food and water bowls. For what reason? He and the other staffers found it amusing to watch the dogs become tipsy. According to sources, the dogs' drinks of choice were gin and whisky. When the queen's staffers found out, King was quickly demoted and given a pay cut. The queen was always away from Buckingham Palace when the pooches were given alcohol.

An Odyssey Uncovered

2001: A Space Odyssey is one of Stanley Kubrick's most iconic movies. Over forty years after the film was released, in 2010, seventeen missing minutes of footage from the film were found in storage at a Kansas salt mine. To this day, no one other than the special effects supervisor and several others working on the film has seen those missing scenes, with one exception. The scenes were included in the film's initial premiere, and then Kubrick removed them to allow for a better flow throughout the film.

Skydiving Adventures

In September of 1999, 47-year-old Joan Murray decided to go on a skydiving adventure. This was nothing out of the ordinary for Murray, who was a thrill seeker and had already been skydiving over 30 times. On this particular day, Murray's main parachute failed to activate, and she was just 700 feet from the ground when she opened her secondary parachute. Her panic caused her to spin around in circles, which landed her right on top of a breeding mound for fire ants. Hundreds of fire ants swarmed her.

While fire ants can cause a deadly allergic reaction, in this case, they saved Murray's life. The stings shocked her heart and kept her heart beating while also stimulating her nerves. Doctors believe that she may have not survived had she landed elsewhere. Murray survived a two-week coma and shattered right leg, but, over the course of two years made a full recovery. How did she celebrate? She went skydiving yet again.

How Strong It Is

If you've ever suffered from heartburn or stomach acid, you know painful it can be. What most people don't realize is that the acid is powerful in more ways than just causing discomfort. The stomach acid in your body is strong enough that it could destroy metal. On the pH scale from 0-14, 0 is the most acidic, 7 is neutral, and 14 is the most basic (non-acidic). Stomach acid generally falls somewhere in the 1-3 range, which is the same area in which you would find battery acid. Who needs superpowers? Your stomach acid can melt metal and eat through wood.

Canary Girls

During World War I, many women left their home and worked in factories on assembly lines to support war efforts. Because of the chemicals they were exposed to, the women on these lines had their hair and skin stained yellow. This earned them the nickname of "Canary Girls". This job involved filling shells with trinitrotoluene, or TNS. The women had to pack the casings with powder then place a detonator in the top. If they pressed too hard, it could detonate. Women lost fingers, hands, and vision, so the yellow skin coloring was seen as the least of their worries. Many agreed that because of the exposure to the chemicals the women looked like canaries, with the stains turning their hair blond and pigmenting their skin. It is even said that some of the women gave birth to babies with yellow skin.

Cheese, Cheese, Cheese

Cheese has been a favorite dairy product for nearly 4,000 years, when people started processing milk from their animals. Today, over 1,770 kinds of cheese exist. Beyond your basic American, mozzarella, Swiss, feta, cheddar, parmesan, and provolone cheeses, there are tons of cheeses most people have never even heard of. Some of these not-so-popular cheeses include Adelost, a blue cheese from Sweden, Carrot Rebel, a carrot-flavored cheese from Austria, Grana Padano, a hard cheese from Italy, and Prairie Tomme, a sheep's milk cheese with a nutty flavor from Missouri.

For some strange cheese names, check out Table Rock, an artisan cheese from Oregon, Nut Rebel, a sweet cow's milk cheese from Austria, Big Woods Blue, a firm cheese from Minnesota, and Cornish Smuggler, a cheddar-style cheese from England. Xynotyro, a hard, Greek cheese, is the only variety of cheese to start with the letter "X". There is only one type of cheese, Goutu, that originates in Swaziland, and one type, Paneer, that originates in Bangladesh.

Alan Smithee

Alan Smithee is a name that no person wants to see listed as the director of a movie they're seeing. He was known for making horrible movies that were poorly-received, ranging from *Death of a Gunfighter* in 1969 to an extended cut of *Dune* in 1984. Why is he still making movies then? It's simple… Alan Smithee is not one single person.

Alan Smithee, sometimes also referred to as "Allen Smithee" is a pseudonym that has been adapted by directors who no longer want to be connected to a film they directed. The pseudonym came into play for *Death of a Gunfighter*, when the director of the film switched halfway through and was replaced with another director. Neither director wanted their name to be listed, so this fictional director was born.

There have been articles and books about the mystery surrounding Smithee's legacy, mostly focusing on how directors' reputations are so important to them that it is worth it to them to give up credit for a piece of their work. The Directors Guild must make a decision regarding each request for use of Alan Smithee as the director's name on a film. The use of the pseudonym was discontinued in 2000, after being used for dozens of films, television movies, and music videos.

Double Bombing Survivor

When the bombs fell on Hiroshima and Nagasaki in 1945, one man had the misfortune of being in both places during both occurrences. Tsutomu Yamaguchi was getting off a trolley on the morning of August 6th when he saw parachutes coming from an airplane. He was less than two miles away when the bomb detonated, and the shock waves ruptured his ear drums. Yamaguchi lost consciousness but eventually awoke and found several of his colleagues.

Together, Yamaguchi and his colleagues made the

nearly 180-mile trip back to their home in Nagasaki. There, he was treated for his injuries and returned to work three days after the explosion. When he explained his experience to his boss and colleagues, they were both amazed and confused. Just as they began to doubt his story—specifically how a single bomb could destroy an entire city—a flash of light filled the room.

It was the second bomb. By some miracle, Yamaguchi, his wife, and his son all survived the explosion. His house, unfortunately, did not. It is said that Yamaguchi is one of 160 people that survived both bombings, but he is the only person recognized by the government as an official "enijuu hibakusha", which means "double bomb survivor."

A Giant Expense

Climbing Mount Everest is not only an investment of livelihood and health, but also of finances. It is estimated that it costs, at minimum, $20,000 to climb the world's most popular peak, but most climbers spend closer to $45,000. The permits alone can range from $7,000 to $10,000 per climber, depending on group size, country, and trek dates. There is also the option for guided and custom climbs, which can hit upwards of $115,000.

The breakdown of expenses varies greatly from person to person. Some people can travel to Nepal for just hundreds of dollars, while roundtrip flights from places like the United States and Australia can cost $5,000 or $7,000. Once climbers land in Kathmandu, they have to take a second flight to Lhasa or Lukla, depending on where they plan on starting their climb. Taxis are scarce in the area, and most climbers take yaks to and from their base camps. These can cost about $40 per day, per yak.

Permit and Sherpa prices vary, but taking a Nepalese Sherpa can cost climbers an additional $6,000-$8,000, when factoring in their salary and work permits. There are also some standard fees for all climbers, such as weather fees, garbage and human waste deposits, and medical support fees. All of these expenses come without factoring in gear. Supplemental oxygen can cost about $500-$600 per bottle, and a mask and regulator will cost another thousand dollars. Tents, cooks, food, fuel, and medical kits also add up quickly. While a climb can be done for $20,000 or so, typical prices from climbing companies and given by past climbers are closer to $40,000-$50,000.

Sourtoe Cocktail

The Yukon Territory in Canada is known for its festivals, hunting opportunities, and view of the northern lights. It's also home to one of the most memorable—and disgusting—cocktails. The Sourtoe Cocktail was invented in 1973, and, unfortunately, it's exactly what you might expect from the name. A human toe is preserved in salt to be used as garnish for any drink you choose.

The story goes that the first toe belonged to a miner named Louie Liken, who had his toe amputated after it was frostbitten. Fifty years later, the toe was found while someone was cleaning out his cabin. Captain Dick Stevenson, the discoverer of the toe, brought it to the local saloon and started placing it in people's drinks. This brought about the formation of the Sourtoe Cocktail Club. The same toe was used for seven more years until a man trying to break a record swallowed the toe.

Seven more toes have since been donated for use, by amputees and anonymous donors. One toe was even dropped off to the Sourdough Saloon with a note that warned people not to mow their lawns in sandals. The only rule of the drink, regardless of which alcohol you choose, is that your lips have to touch the toe, and there is a $2,500 fine in effect for anyone who deliberately consumes the toe.

Melodies & Codes

In mountainous areas and valleys, groups of people all over the world speak in whistles. They call across farms in their whistle language, and men who are courting women whistle their favorite poems to them. There are over 70 different groups in the world who communicate through whistles the same way most other groups communicate with speech.

Whistled tones are used because they are convenient for certain groups, as they can travel up to five miles in the proper conditions.

Inside a Helmet

Astronaut helmets have to have it all—protection, functionality, and support. A standard astronaut helmet has four main components: a neck ring, a protective shell, a feed port, and a vent pad. Made of polycarbonate, the helmets have built-in cameras to send a constant video feed and the neck ring to seal the pressure. The feed port allows for water and food probes.

Astronauts don't have many of the luxuries people often take for granted. If they have an itch on their face, they can't simply take off their helmet to scratch it. Instead, they have a patch of Velcro on the inside of their helmet to remedy the itch. When they want to move their heads, they have to hold onto the helmet to look in a different direction. If this all wasn't enough, the helmet also has components to offer protection from radiation and micrometeoroids.

A Very Thanksgiving Insemination

That turkey at your Thanksgiving table probably didn't come about in the way you might guess. Thanksgiving is all about turkey, so it's no wonder that people search for the biggest turkey possible to feed their families and friends. Believe it or not, this has had an impact on turkey reproduction. In the 1950s, broad-breasted turkeys became more popular than traditional turkeys. These turkeys grow faster—and bigger—than regular turkeys.

Because the turkeys have large breasts, they get in the way when it comes time to reproduce. A combination of this logistical issue and the demand for broad-breasted turkeys has resulted in one solution: artificial insemination. A team secures the male semen from the breeding turkey, called a tom, then bring the contribution into the hen house for insemination. This is a process that takes place year-round to keep up with the demand for turkey.

Quite the Scare

Today, movies like *Scream* and *The Shining* top all the lists of the scariest movies of all time. Back in the 1940s, there was another movie that made waves as a scary movie. *Bambi* came out in 1942, and, as it was following popular Disney movies like *Pinocchio, Dumbo,* and *Snow White and the Seven Dwarfs,* parents were excited to take their kids to see it. However, children at the theaters were traumatized by the death of Bambi's mother, and the danger that remained in the forest throughout the film scared many of them. To this day, it's listed amongst the scariest Disney movies, and the scene of Bambi's mother's death is considered one of the most tragic moments in animated movie history. An animated flick about a fawn is a far cry from today's definition of a "scary movie", but it was traumatic for viewers nonetheless.

Something About a Sloth

Sloths are interesting creatures, to say the least. They are one of those species that everyone knows about but no one knows much about. For starters, most of them walk on the sides of their hind legs. They are capable of standing on two legs, but they generally prefer to walk around on all fours. Scientists divide sloths who live primarily on the ground into four subcategories, three of which walk on the outer sides of their hind feet. The other group, the megalonychids, stand on their back feet, with their walk resembling how humans walk.

Thomas Jefferson, the third president of the United States, had an understated importance in paleontology. Jefferson was sent some bones in 1796, and, instead of disregarding them, spoke about them at a meeting of the American Philosophical Society and eventually named the creature from which the bones came *Megalonyx*. Years later, it was determined that the *Megalonyx* was actually just a flat-footed sloth. One of the species is now named *Magalonyx jeffersonii* in Thomas Jefferson's honor. It is also the official state fossil of West Virginia, where the bones were found.

Today, there are only six living species of sloths, all

fairly similar in size. But, if you look back thousands—or possibly millions— of years, it was a very different picture. The *Megatherium americanum,* which means "giant beast" was the biggest sloth of all time. It was found in South America, and it was the size of an elephant. This creature was up to 20 feet long, and 12 feet tall when standing on its hind legs. Another similar creature was the *Eremotherium,* which could be found in the United States and weighed in around 6,000 pounds. Many of the larger species of sloths also used their tail, which was extremely muscular, as a third leg, when standing up on their hind legs.

In those days, thousands of years ago, it is believed that sloths were a common food amongst humans. There was no proof of this until a sloth fossil that was found in 2008 showed evidence of cuts made by manmade tools. Rewind a few million years, and sloths were also sea-dwellers. These sloths, from the *Thalassocnus* genus, dove into the sea for food, which, over time, evolved into newer sloth species having denser ribs and limbs.

For nearly 11,000 years, there have been no indigenous sloth species on North America. Five hundred years after sloths in North America became extinct, indigenous sloths in South America also became extinct.

Name A Hurricane

Up until 1950, hurricane names had no rhythm or method. They were often names based off of the location or year of their occurrence, like the Miami Hurricane of 1926 or the Sea Islands Hurricane in 1893, and only the largest, most destructive storms were given names. In 1950, naming the storms began, and they were taken from the Joint Army/Navy Phonetic Alphabet.

The first hurricane season with this new naming rule saw storms like Hurricane Love and Hurricane Dog. For two more years, this naming system carried on, until it was decided that reusing the same list of names each year would cause problems and confusion. After all, there was a Hurricane Able in 1950, 1951, *and* 1952. Finally, in 1953, the United States National Hurricane Center decided to start using female names, explaining that this would cause less confusion.

This concept of naming storms after humans made it easier to spread awareness and helped capture the attention of the general public. It gave them something to associate with the incoming storm. The names of these storms often came from the names of forecasters' wives, until men's names were added to the list of possibilities in 1979. Now, there are six master lists that are rotated annually, meaning that names of storms repeat every six years. The names alternate between male and female and vary based on region.

Names of storms that result in extreme devastation or loss of lives are generally retired as a way to honor the victims and dissociate painful memories. Such storms include Hurricane Irene, Hurricane Sandy, Hurricane Katrina, and Hurricane Andrew. Seventy-eight names of Atlantic hurricanes have been retired since 1954.

Take Me to Church

The Euclid Square mall in Euclid, Ohio, first opened its doors in 1977 with around 100 stores. Thirty-four years later, only sixteen stores remained, including a pizza shop, a men's clothing store, and several boutiques. By 2003, the only store left was a Dillard's clearance store. The mall found a new sense of purpose in the mid-2000s, in the form of faith and spirituality.

Twenty-four church congregations rented out store space in the Euclid mall as a place to hold their Sunday worship services. Rent generally cost about $500 to $1,000 per month, and the leases were on a month-to-month basis. Many of the churches used the mall as a starting point to build up their congregations until they could afford a building of their own.

Where the Foot Locker used to be, there was Grace and Mercy Church of the Living God. Where Dollar Tree once stood, you could find God's Way Gospel

Church in 2004. A former Fashion Bug was converted into Crown of Life. While the congregations' locations may have seemed unconventional, congregants said that it doesn't matter where the church is, as long as they can worship together.

The final Dillard's store closed in September 2013 once its lease was finished, and the mall itself was closed down permanently in late 2016. Many of the churches have found other buildings to call home, and there are now plans to tear down the building that was once a popular mall and start fresh with a new office complex.

Sun Owner?

In 2010, a woman from Vigo, Spain, made a startling accusation: that she was the owner of the sun. Angeles Duran had applied for ownership of the sun after learning that an American had made similar clams on the moon and Mars. There is already an official treaty, the Outer Space Treaty of 1967, that prevents governments from claiming ownership of celestial bodies, but there is nothing that legally keeps individuals from staking claim. Duran asserted that she was issued a document that stated that she was the owner of the sun and stated that she knew the laws surrounding the idea and met with lawyers, who backed her idea. She says that anyone else could have claimed the right, but that she was simply the first to think of it. Duran wanted to charge "rent" for everyone who used the sun's energy, and said that she would distribute the earnings amongst the government, a pension fund, charity, and herself.

Rock Stars & Babies

Some people love heavy metal music, while others can't stand it. Either way, there is no denying that there is strategy and method to such singing. Krzysztof Izdebski is a doctor that works for the Pacific Voice and Speech Foundation, and he made it his mission to find out why phonotrauma, vocal cord bleeding and straining, occurs to some people, but not often heavy metal singers.

Dr. Izbeski used a high-speed camera designed to analyze vocal cords and record videos of throats in action. Through his research, Izdebski found that, when heavy metal singers sing, their vocal cords don't touch one another. This is unlike typical screaming, but very similar to another occurrence: baby crying and screaming. Like babies, heavy metal singers aren't damaging their vocal cords, as the instinct is to open the muscles in a way that air is pushed through the vocal cords.

Hatespeare

William Shakespeare is known for his iconic works, like *Julius Caesar*, *Othello,* and *Hamlet.* Students read his plays and stories all over the world, but some of the world's most famous writers aren't quite as fond of his writing. Leo Tolstoy, writer of *War and Peace*, wrote a 100-page critique of Shakespeare and his plays. The essay was published in 1906 and called Shakespeare's work "trivial, and positively bad". Tolstoy said that he first read many of the works, like *Romeo and Juliet* and *Macbeth*, in school for the first time, and felt repulsed by then. Even at age 75, he said that he re-read the works and felt just as strongly about Shakespeare's writing.

The Times ranked J.R.R. Tolkien as one of the greatest British authors. Before the days of *The Lord of the Rings*, a teenaged Tolkien delivered a speech on why Shakespeare's work didn't deserve the praise it received, and he later on referred to it as "folly or foolish. Similarly, George Bernard Shaw was a theater critic for a newspaper in London before his own career took off. He said that there was no writer that he disliked as much as he disliked Shakespeare. He reviewed over fifteen of Shakespeare's works during his three years as a theater critic, calling *Othello* "melodramatic" and referring to Shakespeare's writing as incoherent.

Robert Greene was a popular Elizabethan playwright who lived during Shakespeare's time. He was also one of Shakespeare's most notable critics. He was displeased that Shakespeare had started off as an actor and dared to switch to writing plays. Several decades later, Samuel Pepys echoed the sentiment. Pepys was a notable diarist in the 1600s and, after attending a performance of *A Midsummer Night's Dream*, called the play insipid and ridiculous.

No Sleep Tonight

There are all sorts of world records that have been set, but some cause more problems than others. In 1964, a high school student set the world record for longest time staying awake. Seventeen-year-old Randy Gardner stayed awake for 11 days straight as part of a science project. Gardner used no stimulants or other medications, relying only on his friends to help keep him awake. The record before him was set by a radio disc jockey in 1959 as part of a publicity tactic for his radio station.

Years later, Gardner told the press that his only motivation to attempt this record was to win the school science fair. Since 1964, there have been other people who have claimed to break Gardner's record. Maureen Weston, a woman from the United Kingdom, is one that was observed and officially broke the record, staying up for 449 hours straight. She was featured in the 1978 Guinness Book of World Records. Randy Gardner still makes headlines as the one who broke the world record, mostly because he caught the attention of the press and a renowned sleep researcher.

Despite the efforts of many, Guinness has decided to no longer include sleep deprivation among their records due to possible health risks. Several of those who attempted—and broke—the world record admitted to having hallucinations and paranoia throughout their sleepless days and nights.

Duck Tales

If you're on the shores of Alaska and happen to see a rubber duck wash onto shore, it's not a prank or strange coincidence. It's actually part of a global phenomenon that has since been forgotten by many. In 1992, a crate fell overboard from a ship on its way to the United States from Hong Kong. The contents? 28,000 plastic rubber duck toys. Over twenty years later, some of these ducks are still floating around in the ocean. They have been found all over the world from Hawaii to South America, to the Pacific Northwest. Some have been frozen in ice, while others have washed onto beaches.

There is even a group of followers, the "Friendly Floatees", that devote themselves to tracking where these rubber ducks have floated to. To this day, there are 2,000 of the toys that have remained close together, caught up in the currents near Japan and southeast Alaska, called the North Pacific Gyre. This situation has even helped scientists understand more about ocean currents and pollution.

For those enthralled by the displacement of bath toys, there is a book by Donovan Hahn that chronicles the story of these 28,000 rubber ducks, entitled *Moby-Duck: The True Story of 28,000 Bath Toys*

Lost at Sea & of the Beachcombers, Oceanographers, Environmentalists, and Fools, Including the Author, Who Went in Search of Them.

Catch A Tase

Taser guns have been carried by many law enforcement officers for years. In 1993, a unique system, AFID, was created to take Tasers to the next level. AFID, or anti-felon identification, tags look like colorful confetti that is fired from the Taser guns. In reality, these tiny tags have microscopic serial numbers. These numbers are used to help track where the "confetti" came from and who fired it. While not all Taser guns have this feature, it is becoming increasingly popular, as it prevents the misuse of Taser guns and allows for extra accountability.

The General of the Chicken

You'd be hard-pressed to find a Chinese restaurant in the United States without General Tso's (also called General Zuo's) chicken on the menu. However, if you take a visit to Hunan, a province in China, you'd be hard-pressed to find someone who has even heard of the dish. General Tso's chicken is an Americanized Chinese food dish consisting of battered chicken in a sweet and spicy sauce. But how did the dish get its name, and where did it come from?

Tso Tsung-t'ang, also known as Zuo Zongtang, was

a general in the 19th century, and legend says that he enjoyed eating the dish. He was part of the military administration through the Qing dynasty and is known for his capturing of the desert region of Xinjiang. General Tsung-t'ang helped recapture the land from the Uyghur Muslims. No one knows how this honored man became the inspiration behind the Chinese food dish we've all come to know and love.

The story goes that a notable chef, Peng Chang-kuei, had previously cooked for the general, but when he was asked in New York in the 1970s to make the meal he had made for the general, he could not quite remember. He created what is now known as General Tso's chicken, which is said to be very different from the original General Tso's chicken, which had no sugar and tasted more like traditional Hunanese cuisine. However, the dish caught on and was imitated by many. Although it is touted as a historical dish that comes right from Hunan, it was invented in America less than a half century ago.

Mind Your Own Sand

Villages in India rely on rivers, which in turn rely on sand to act as a regulator of the river's flow. However, in recent years, India has had a large problem with sand thieves. Locals refer to the people involved in this thievery as "sand mafia", as it is believed that capitalists, mobsters, and politicians are all a part of covering up the issue. Sand is a large part of making concrete, and the focus in India has more recently turned to urbanization. Sand has been taken to use in the building of bridges, skyscrapers, and apartment buildings.

This has had a massive impact on villages around the rivers. The taking of the sand has resulted in a drop of the water table, and wells have begun to dry up. It has also washed the water out of rice paddies, the designated land areas used to grow rice. Bridges even run the risk of collapsing, as a result of the weakened foundations due to lack of sand. What most people don't realize is that India uses sand as a main construction material, as it is versatile, strong, and cheap. It is debated amongst the locals whether the benefits of using sand to build are worth the problems they are causing. From the outside, fighting over sand seems silly. In reality, it's a large part of everyday life in other countries.

Ring Finders

The Ring Finders is a service and website that has been around for over two decades. It serves one single purpose: to find lost wedding rings and engagement rings. The company boasts that, as of October 2016, they have made nearly 3,000 recoveries. The Ring Finders was created by Chris Turner, a Vancouver native who, at the age of 13, helped his neighbor find her wedding ring that had been missing for ten years. Turner had received a metal detector and found the ring that his neighbor had lost gardening. He continued helping others find their lost treasures, which gave him the idea to start the business.

Members pay a fee to belong on the Ring Finders site, which allows them to match up with people who need their expertise. There are currently ring finding experts in 25 countries who make it their mission to help people find their lost items. The jewelry is found using metal detectors, so it targets those who know that they lost their ring in a particular area, such as a beach or a park. One success story the company shares is centered on Tim, a newlywed who lost his ring while swimming at the beach in South Carolina. He and his wife got in touch with a local member of Ring Finders, who found the ring in less than ten minutes. Talk about a gem of a business.

A Strange Start

Matt Dillon was a typical middle school student in Westchester, New York when he was discovered in 1978. Casting directors were visiting local middle schools, looking for fresh-faced talent to star in a new movie. They would go from one classroom to another, asking questions to any student who they felt seemed interesting or had the look they were seeking. At Hommocks Middle School, Matt Dillon was cutting class, walking through the hallways, trying to put out a tough-guy image. The talent scout who first met him commented that he was trying hard to seem like a bad kid from the wrong side of town, and eventually found out he was from a middle-class family in a great area.

The film he was cast for? *Over the Edge,* a drama about teenagers in the 1970s. Dillon received a positive response, which led to him being cast in *My Bodyguard*, another film that got great reviews and solidified his reputation as a teen icon. He starred in over five major films in the five years following his initial discovery. Dillon has gone on to star in popular movies like *There's Something About Mary* and *Beautiful Girls* and was nominated for an Academy Award and Golden Globe for his role in *Crash.* Imagine if he had decided to go to class that day in middle school.

Getting Higher

The Doors were icons in the 1960s and 1970s, but not everyone appreciated their music as it was. Jim Morrison, the lead singer, was known for being unpredictable, so Ed Sullivan made sure to meet with the band ahead of their performance on *Ed Sullivan Show* in September 1967. The show's host had one simple request: change the lyrics of their song "Light My Fire" from "We couldn't get much higher" to "We couldn't get much better." Morrison sang the lyric as it was originally written, much to the dismay of Ed Sullivan. Instead of inviting the group back for six more shows as producers had originally planned, he banned them from ever performing on the show in the future.

Women Soldiers

Society has a vision of how soldiers should look, but parts of the world haven't always felt the same way. During World War I, nearly six thousand women served in Russia's military, making it the only country at the time to allow women to serve in gender-segregated formations. It was common in the early 1900s for women to disguise themselves as men so they would be allowed to serve in the military. These women were from all different backgrounds, and some even used their social influence to enter the army and serve alongside their family members.

In Russia's Great War, the first all-female units were formed. Women wanted to play a larger role on the frontlines, and a woman from Siberia, Maria Bochkareva, was the one who ultimately secured permission from the Minister of War to organize all-female units in the military. These groups included the 1st Russian Women's Battalion of Death, the 1st Petrograd Women's Battalion, and the 2nd Moscow Women's Battalion of Death. The women's units were ultimately disbanded in November of 1917.

Drinking for Cheap

Forty years ago, there were just 89 breweries in the United States. Today, there are over 2,500 breweries. The competition is more existent than ever. Craft beer has spread from the West Coast to all over the

US, and beers like Keystone and Dogfish Head 90 Minute can be found anywhere. Cheap, widely-distributed beers are still amongst the most popular beers in the United States this year, with Bud Light, Coors Light, Miller Lite, and Budweiser topping the list of bestsellers.

More Than a Political Agenda

Gary Hart entered the presidential race in the late 1980s hoping to make a legacy for himself. He was a frontrunner against all other Democratic candidates, and, in a projected election against then-Vice President George H.W. Bush, was garnering over 50% of votes. Hart's campaign for presidency took a very different turn with one of the first publicized political affairs.

Hart was suspected of having an affair with Donna Rice, a woman nearly half his age, around the same time he was campaigning for the presidency. They were photographed together on a yacht, notably called Monkey Business, and news of their cruise together becoming public along with an anonymous call to the Miami Herald, is what started Hart's downfall. The caller, never identified but presumed to be a friend of Donna Rice's, gave the date and location of a planned meet between Hart and Rice, which brought the affair into the spotlight.

Affairs have become somewhat of a normal occurrence in the world of celebrity and politics, but that wasn't quite the case in Hart's days. This became one of the first—and the most memorable— sex scandals to ever occur during a political campaign. While presidents like Franklin Roosevelt and John F. Kennedy were known for having extramarital affairs, no affair had, up until this point, had such an impact on the outcome of a political figure's endeavors.

The Domino's Plan

Before Domino's was the second-largest pizza restaurant chain in America, it was a small Michigan pizza shop in the 1960s. The chain was founded by two brothers, who also were the brains behind the iconic and ever-recognizable Domino's logo. While the Domino's logo features a domino for obvious reasons, the number of dots on the domino serves a purpose. When the logo was created, there were three original locations, so they opted to have one dot for each location.

The plan was to add another dot each time they opened a new location, but, due to the unforeseen success of the chain, it was deemed impossible. The original Domino's logo was used until 1987, when it was flipped, and the blue and red colors made brighter to capture customers' attention. Finally, in 2012, the current logo was created. This logo took the original domino picture and tilted it, separating the name of the chain from the picture. It also was the first logo to not have the word "pizza" in it. This was to emphasize that they offer a wide selection beyond just pizza. It's a good thing Domino's opted not to go with the original plan of adding a dot for each new location; they would have over 10,000 dots to fit in.

Saving Lives in Soccer

Francis Koné is pretty busy these days. In addition to playing for the 1. FC Slovacko soccer team, he has saved four lives in the soccer world during his eight-year career. Most recently, Koné's team was versing Bohemians 1905 in Prague, when the defender collided with the goalie from the opposite team. While the defender got up, the goalie was lying on his back, unconscious. Koné's quick thinking led him to open the goalie's mouth and hold his tongue to make sure he didn't swallow it. He made sure the airways were clear and stayed alongside the goalie's teammates until he regained consciousness.

When Koné was first starting out in professional soccer, he aided a teammate who collapsed in the gym in Thailand. Another time, a player crashed into a goalkeeper then fell onto his neck. Koné made sure to get his tongue out of his mouth until medics came to help. A similar occurrence happened while Koné was in Africa in 2015. Talk about some good luck — or is it bad luck?

Smarter Than Maps

In a time full of navigation apps and GPS systems, one group of people is being told not to rely on the technology. Cab drivers in London are required to learn all of the roads in their area, as well as the fastest ways to get to every location. More than that, for the past 150 years, all taxi drivers have been required to pass a test. The test taxi drivers must pass is called "The Knowledge", and it requires learning at least 300 basic routes, 25,000 streets, and over 15,000 landmarks and notable locations. It takes, on average, three or four years for a driver to learn the entirety of "The Knowledge". The recent popularity of navigation systems and services like Uber have taken over, but taxi drivers have become more of an experience than a service in London. These drivers know the routes, the history, and the landmarks of their entire city.

Seven Continents of Shows

Metallica is amongst the most popular bands in the world. In addition to playing sold-out shows all over the United States, Asia, and Europe, the band set out on another mission: to play a show on every continent. With one continent left to check off, in 2013, the members of Metallica traveled to Antarctica to play a show in a small dome for just 120 people. The audience was made up of research scientists from countries like Russia, China, Poland,

and Chile, as well as several contest winners from Latin America.

The band had to play the show without any amplification in order to preserve the fragile exterior environment, and the sound was transmitted through headphones. Metallica's ten-song show was the second rock concert to ever take place on Antarctica, the first being performed by a team of scientists that formed a band called Nunatak.

Unlikely Pals

Julia Grant was married to Ulysses S. Grant, who served as the president of the United States from 1869 to 1877. Varina Davis was married to Jefferson Davis, the first and only president of the Confederate States of America during the Civil War. The two were extremely similar, both born in 1826 and following in their husbands' lofty aspirations, but they lived in two completely different worlds.

Julia's husband was the commander of the Union army, while Varina's husband led the opposing side. Julia had a strong, solid marriage with her husband, and thoroughly enjoyed being the First Lady. She spoke highly of her husband and maintained friendships with many presidents' wives. The Davises, on the other hand, had an unfulfilling marriage and very different opinions on his presidency of the Confederacy.

It wasn't until several years after both husbands had

died that the two women finally met in 1893. Despite coming from opposite sides, they became great friends. They traveled together, dined together, and had their daughters spend a great deal of time together. Both had caused some controversy during their husbands' time in office—Varina, for coming off as rude, and Julia for being thought of as overly influential in her husband's decisions. This was simply another aspect of life for them to bond over. Toward the end of their lives, Julia Grant and Varina Davis even had small cottages on nearby lots and saw each other on a daily basis. It was a friendship that surprised historians for decades.

Colors and Copyright

While trademarks and copyright protect company names and logos, there's a special kind of copyright to protect colors. It wasn't until 1985 that the first rulings were made in regard to color trademarks. Color trademarks are more difficult to obtain, and they oftentimes only apply to a certain sector. For example, Cadbury has a particular shade of purple it is recognized for. No other company can use this exact purple for chocolate products, but they can use it for anything from shoe lines to nutritional supplements. The general rule of thumb is that the color must be so strongly associated with the brand by the general public that it would not be functional for other companies to use.

All John Deere products have that same recognizable

color of green, but the color itself is not protected. Their logo, consisting of a yellow deer with the green background, is trademarked, but other farmers, trailer companies, and field workers can paint their equipment the same color. The same goes for McDonald's. Despite the red and yellow coloration of the logo being easily distinguishable as theirs, any company can use those colors. The trouble comes if they try to have a design involving a yellow arch and red background. There can be another burger chain that tries to use the same exact colors McDonald's uses in their logo, but unless they use the same design, they are free and clear to do so.

Some companies have coverage on certain aspects, but not all of their products. Tiffany Blue, the robin's egg blue color you see on every Tiffany bag or box, is a color that is trademarked for those purposes specifically. Their color trademark only applies to their packaging, and other companies can use robin's egg blue for any other purpose. There are companies that have failed to obtain color copyright for their products, like pink for Pepto-Bismol and white for Good Humor.

Pitcairn

Who doesn't love a nice tropical vacation?! Pitcairn is an island in the Pacific with a land area of about 2 square miles, and it's one of the fourteen British territories that remain overseas. Over time, the population has dwindled down to a mere 50 inhabitants. That's right, there are less than 50 people who live on the entire island.

As a way to try to attract new inhabitants, the government of Pitcairn has been offering a free plot of land to each person who chooses to move to the island. So far, a mere one person has taken them up on the offer. There's a catch, though. The island isn't exactly modernized. While they finally got electricity and internet on Pitcairn, there is just one store on the island, and it is open only three times a week. Shipments of food from New Zealand come in three times a year. If you're looking for warm weather, clear, blue water, and a slower-paced life, you could be the next resident of Pitcairn Island.

German Enlargement Plans

It is estimated that in 2013, a whopping 15,414 men had penis enlargement procedures performed. Of those men, nearly 15% of them came from Germany. The country with the second-largest number of enlargement procedures performed was nowhere close to Germany's number. 473 Venezuelan men had the penis enlargement operation done, as did 471 Spanish men and 295 Mexican men.

The trend of growth in the penis enlargement industry was first noticed in 2011, and it is now said that the enlargement surgery is the seventh most popular cosmetic or aesthetic surgery amongst men in Germany. Worldwide, it is still behind at least sixteen other types of cosmetic surgeries. Breast augmentations, liposuctions, eyelid surgeries, and lipostructure procedures were all performed over one million times in 2013.

The Mummy Stories

While mummies are normally thought of as humans, it was also common for Egyptians to mummify animals. This was for a variety of reasons. Sometimes, animals were brought in the home to live as pets, and they were mummified when they died and were buried. Other times, animals were mummified to be sacrificed or offered to humans for the afterlife. When animals were mummified in ancient Egypt as a sacrifice, they were able to be bartered or purchased. It is believed, after studying mummified animals, that partial remains like feathers from birds were sold instead of full animals. Over thirty catacombs have been found filled with mummies, all dedicated to one particular animal. All types of animals, ranging from crocodiles to cats, have been found in mummified form.

Requirements Unlike Any Other

In 2012, the China Defense Mashup (CDM) was searching for two female astronauts to take part in the Shenzhou-9 mission. The statement released said that they were seeking women who were married, had no scars or rotten teeth, and had given birth naturally. They went further and proclaimed that they were looking for "flawless" women to partake in this mission. Their reasoning was that scars could start bleeding and decayed teeth could cause problems. They also said that body odor was not allowed, as the limited space would only cause it to intensify. Talk about some unique specifications.

Texhoma

On the border of Texas and Oklahoma lies a town called—you guessed it—Texhoma. Texhoma is home to 926 residents, a sharp decline from the 1,464 residents who inhabited the town sixty years ago. The town's demographics have long been measured separately by both states. In 1990, the Oklahoma section of Texhoma had 746 residents, while the Texas section had 291. A law was passed in both the Oklahoma and Texas state legislatures that allowed a school district to cover the border of both states.

For most of the 1970s, kindergarten and middle school were handled by a Texas school board, while elementary school and high school were handed by an Oklahoma school board. Eventually, this was overturned, and Texas serves kindergarten through fourth grade, while Oklahoma serves fifth through twelfth grade. Students, whether they're from Texhoma, Texas, or Texhoma, Oklahoma, can attend public colleges in each state with in-state tuition fees.

Frozen in Time

In 2016, a 14-year-old girl in England made history when she was awarded the right to be cryogenically frozen. The girl, whose name was never released, was dying of cancer, and she wanted to have her body frozen in case scientists ever made new discoveries that would bring her back to life or cure her disease. Her father initially did not support her wishes until she got a lawyer involved. As the girl was too young to make a will, she requested that her mom, who supported her wishes to be cryogenically frozen, be given sole responsibility for making decisions on her behalf.

The girl wrote a letter to the court saying that she didn't want to be buried underground, and that she wanted another chance at life. The judge ruled that, despite cryogenic technology not yet being proven as effective, the girl was in her right mind to make the decision. The facility that would house her body cost approximately $46,000, but she made it her final wish to be frozen. She died shortly thereafter, and her body was sent to a cryogenic storage facility.

Secrets About Bono

Bono is known around the world, but he grew up in Ireland as Paul Hewson. His stage name came about when he was hanging on the streets with friends as a teenager. They called him "Bono Vox" after a local hearing aid store, and it was shortened to Bono. It stuck with him from then on. Known as the lead singer of U2, Bono has accomplished much more than simply recording albums, writing music, and touring. He is the only person to have been nominated for an Oscar, a Grammy, a Golden Globe, *and* a Nobel Peace Prize, having won 22 Grammys with U2. More than that, he has appeared in multiple films, co-written feature films, and made a name for himself as one of the most philanthropic celebrities in Hollywood. However, don't ask Bono about his band name; it turns out that he isn't actually fond of the name U2. The band was initially called Feedback, but their album sleeve designer suggested U2.

Cow Time

Tons of plans, ideas, and schemes for avoiding or reducing taxes owed have been an undeniable part of society for years. One group of people in Florida has come up with a unique way to beat the system. Florida has what's called a greenbelt law, which allows for lower taxation rates of farmland in an effort to support agriculture. It dates back to the 1950s, when swamplands were being converted into commercial areas because owners couldn't afford the taxes. The only current limit is that the greenbelt law does not apply to residential areas. Why? People were simply buying a few sheep or cows to keep on their property in order to save money.

One thing is being done that is definitely out of the

ordinary: renting cows. It's not exactly what it sounds like, but it definitely is a unique way to bend the rules. These people, generally businesses, can avoid paying the higher tax rate simply by keeping some livestock on their property. This loophole got the nickname of "rent-a-cow" because the land owners will actually often pay the ranchers to keep their cows on their property. Walt Disney World is one of the most notable partakers in this loophole, and it is estimated that it has saved them over a million dollars. Reform efforts have been made, but nothing has stuck. Lawmakers are hesitant to make any changes because, despite this law costing the state hundreds of millions of dollars each year, it is hard to know where to draw the line and how it would impact any actual farmers.

True Lies

The 1994 film True Lies had an all-star cast: Arnold Schwarzenegger, Jamie Lee Curtis, and Eliza Dushku. It also had an all-star budget. With a production budget of over $100 million, the movie was the most expensive movie ever filmed at that time. The three jets used in the film were actual US military fighter jets, and they cost over $100,000 to rent. Lucky for the cast and James Cameron, the producer, the movie saw great commercial success. It garnered several Academy Award nominations, Jamie Lee Curtis won a Golden Globe for her role in the film, and it grossed a worldwide total of $378 million at the box office. Talk about proving the skeptics wrong.

Testicle Festival

Looking for a good time? Amongst the thousands of festivals that take place across the country each year, one will leave you with memories unlike any other. Head out west to the Montana Testicle Festival, an annual event that's been taking place since 1982. Their slogan, "having a ball," is undeniably funny, and they warn that a weekend at the festival will involve "lots of balls." The festival takes place in Clinton, Montana, over the course of five days. A normal day at the festival includes a women's oil wrestling contest, a "big ball" competition, which is said to be the male equivalent of a wet T-shirt contest, and nudists walking around with rings around their penis.

The main event of the Testicle Festival is the bull ball eating competition. Typical food served there? It may look like your average fair food, but it's really fried cow testicles. On average, the attendees eat 600 to 700 pounds of balls each year. Instead of the Indy 500, you can check out the Undie 500, which finds men and women riding tricycles in their underwear. At the very least, there is a philanthropic side to the festival. In 2015, they donated $5,000 to a charity that benefits those battling testicular cancer.

The Library of Tweets

If ever there were an unlikely partnership, it would be between Twitter and the Library of Congress. In 2010, however, they announced that, together, they would archive every tweet that had ever been and would ever be posted. The news was announced over Twitter with a simple Tweet: "Library to acquire ENTIRE Twitter archive—ALL public tweets, ever, since March 2006! Details to follow." It was a big task, but surely something the largest library in the world could handle, right?

It has been seven years since the announcement, but the Library of Congress still has yet to launch the archive of tweets. No schedule has been projected, no engineers have been hired, and no progress has been made. In the meantime, archivists and researchers still pay for a licensing fee in order to receive data from Twitter with the hopes of being able to sift through tweets to learn more about language and societal ideas. With an estimated 500 million tweets being sent into cyber space each day, it remains up in the air if the Library of Congress will ever be able to archive every single tweet. After all, when the deal was made between the two companies, only 55 million posts were being tweeted each day.

Twitter is one of the only social media sites willing to share their data in such a manner. It makes millions of dollars each year from selling such data, and researchers are confident that the continuation of shared data will help learn more about society. In just the first half of 2013, Twitter made $32 million licensing data to a variety of other companies. The Library of Congress continues to say that the Twitter archive project remains a priority for them, and they're also trying to find the best way to update or revise data when tweets are deleted and accounts are made private.

Popes' Past Job

Everyone has had their share of bad jobs. Even one of the most famous religious figures in the world. In December of 2013, Pope Francis was speaking at San Cirillo Alessandrino Church in Rome when he revealed that he used to work as a bouncer. While he was listing his previous jobs, he shared that he worked at a Buenos Aires night club as a bouncer. Other jobs of the pontiff included sweeping floors, teaching, and performing tests in a chemistry lab.

Em Dash

Believe it or not, the mark that looks like two dashes/hyphens put together has a particular name: the em dash. This is not to be confused with the en dash, which is narrower and used for different purposes. The em dash can be used in place of commas, in instances like, "When she got the flowers—almost three weeks after her date—she had already made up her mind that she no longer wished to date him." It can also be used in place of parentheses, but it is considered to be less formal and more intrusive. For added emphasis, the em dash is also used to replace a colon. Most word processors form the em dash when you type two hyphens in a row.

A Mystery Unsolved?

Bobby Dunbar was four years old when he disappeared in Louisiana. It was August of 1912, and his family, from a small town in central Louisiana, had taken a trip to Swayze Lake. Bobby went missing sometime during the fishing trip, and the search for the missing boy began immediately.

Eight months after his disappearance, police found Bobby Dunbar—or a child they believed was Bobby Dunbar—with a man named William Cantwell Walters. Walters maintained that the boy was not Bobby Dunbar but a boy by the name Bruce Anderson, the child of a friend whom he had temporary custody of. Both sets of parents were asked to identify the child. The Dunbars said that the boy was their son, while Bruce's mother admitted she hadn't seen him in 13 months. There are different stories told about the boy's reaction, with some saying he cried upon seeing the Dunbars, and others saying he ran up and yelled, "Mother!" upon seeing Leslie Dunbar. Custody was granted to the Dunbars, with a judge ruling that this boy was, in fact, Bobby Dunbar.

Bruce Anderson's mother had three children out of wedlock, which did not bode well for her in the courtroom. While the law had decided that the boy was Bobby Dunbar, in her mind, her son was being kidnapped by the Dunbars. She consistently maintained that the boy was her son, Bruce. After two years in jail for kidnapping, William Cantwell Walters was released, and the boy was raised as Bobby Dunbar. He got married, had children, and raised his family as a Dunbar.

Years later, in 2004, Bobby's son was curious about the story, so he decided to have a DNA test done. He had his DNA compared to that of his cousin, and it was found that there was no familial match. To this day, no one knows what happened to the actual boy named Bobby Dunbar. There are all sorts of theories, ranging from his parents harming him and taking in the other boy to cover up their crimes, to him being kidnapped and switched by Walters.

Republic of New Atlantis

Ernest Hemingway isn't the only Hemingway worth knowing about. Ernest had a younger brother, Leicester—pronounced as "Lester"—who had his own claim to fame: he founded his own country. In 1964, Leicester was quoted saying to the *Washington Post* that there's no law saying that you can't start your own country, so that's exactly what he did.

Leicester's country was called the Republic of New Atlantis. It was created out of a barge that measured 8-feet by 30-feet. He anchored it to a Ford engine block on a shallow bank about eight miles from Jamaica. Thus, New Atlantis was born. Leicester stated that the Guano Islands of Act of 1856 gave him the right to take possession of any unoccupied "island, rock, or key" on which bird excrements were found, as bird droppings were a valuable fertilizer in those days.

A year after its founding, the seven voters of the country, all chosen by Leicester, elected Leicester Hemingway as their first president. This made headlines all over the world, as New Atlantis shared its official country flag, sewn by Leicester's wife. He even created his own currency, the scruple. Many historians note that the currency looked like it was simply made of articles that had washed ashore. Leicester created a New Atlantis Constitution, which was a near-copy of the beginning of the US Constitution.

Surprisingly, no other countries had a problem with the founding of New Atlantis, and a spokesperson for the Jamaican Embassy even said they thought the project was "sound". Unfortunately, several years after its founding as a country, New Atlantis was washed away in a storm. The University of Texas Research Center created an exhibit with artifacts from the country, including its flag, its postage stamps, and a page of their constitution.

Ain't Nothing but A Coon Dog

Everyone loves their dogs, but one community in Alabama has taken the adoration of these furry friends to the next level. In Cherokee, Alabama, you can find the world's only pet cemetery dedicated solely to coon dogs. The cemetery was founded in 1937 by Key Underwood, who wanted to honor his beloved coon dog, Troop. The property is miles off the beaten path, and there are some lofty requirements in order to get your coon dog buried there.

The Coon Dog Cemetery's website states that the owner must verify the coon dog was, in fact, an authentic coon dog, there must be a witness to verify this, and a member of the Key Underwood Coon Dog Memorial Grave Yard, Inc. must also be allowed the chance to see the coon dog and identify it as such. The graves at the cemetery vary greatly, just like what you would see in any ordinary cemetery. Some headstones are homemade, while others share information like the dog's favorite activities. Walking through the cemetery, you can find a myriad of flowers, flags, and coins left at the graves.

Flat Earth Society

It's been hundreds of years since it was first established that the world was round and not flat. However, there are still tons of people who believe that the world actually is flat. In 2004, the Flat Earth Society was launched, and it began welcoming new members in 2009. These people who believe the Earth is flat are known as "Flat Earthers", and it's simply considered another conspiracy theory. There are various groups and websites working to "raise awareness" and get rid of what they feel is a myth that the world is round. People have created YouTube pages, like a series called Flat Earth Clues, and websites, like Enclosed World, in an effort to spread their theory of the Earth being flat.

Based on A True Story?

Mort Crim, from a small coal-mining town in Illinois, made his name as a newscaster. He became a household name when it was revealed that he served as the inspiration for the Will Ferrell comedy *Anchorman*. Despite the humorous portrayal of his characterizations, Crim says that he isn't offended at all and doesn't regret serving as the inspiration for Ron Burgundy. He initially found out that he was the inspiration for the character in 2003, while Will Ferrell was doing interviews before the first movie came out.

Crim admits that, like Ron Burgundy, he does groom himself quite a bit, but he says that the accusation of him being a "chauvinist pig" is a bit far off the mark. Unlike the character based off him, Crim has no catchy sign-off phrase. The main reason Ferrell created Ron Burgundy as a fictional representation of

Crim? His scuffles with his female co-anchor. Jessica Savitch was his co-anchor on WDIV-TV in Detroit, and one of the first female anchors on television. Multiple sources said that Mort Crim did not treat her well, and when Ferrell found this out, he began creating the character of Ron Burgundy.

Tales of Pirates

Pirates of the Caribbean has become an iconic film franchise since the first film came out in 2003. Filming and producing these movies has brought about some interesting stories. For the second and third films in the series, the crew was so large that snacks alone cost nearly $2 million. They had a chef on set with cast and crew, always ready to serve up snacks and meals. At some points, they used actual boats to transport trailers and crew members to and from St. Vincent, where the movies were being filmed. This required a whopping 55 boats.

Over the course of filming the first three movies, an estimated 240 cell phones ended up in the water at some point. The cast and crew recognize how different the filming experience became from the first film through the most recent film. At the beginning, they used to have to fly in meals. The actors had to go to an actual Pirates School to learn how to use swords and work with cannons. So much for pirates telling no tales.

Table Etiquette for Dummies

You can say a lot by the way you arrange your dishes and utensils on the table or the way you carry yourself at a dinner party. Table etiquette is a language of its own, and all sorts of rules have amassed over the years. If someone wants to take a break from eating, it is customary for them to put the knife and fork with the tips facing one another, almost like an upside-down V. The other formation they can choose is placing their knife diagonally on the top right of their plate, with the fork tines up, lower down on the plate. Technically, if you are leaving your utensils resting in another manner, that is an indication that you are ready for the next course or to have your dish removed. The standard when finished eating is to leave the fork and knife diagonally across the plate, parallel to one another. It is also considered rude to leave your utensils halfway on the plate, halfway on the table.

Another etiquette rule? The first toast at a meal should only be given by the host or hostess at the beginning of the meal. All other toasts should be saved until the start of the dessert course. While in movies or in past experiences you might have seen people clinking their glasses with utensils in an effort to get everyone's attention before a toast or speech, this is considered to be inappropriate. If a particular guest is being toasted, they should not stand up or drink to themselves.

It is also, in proper dinner etiquette, seen as rude or improper to order a different number of courses as your dining companions, just as it is considered rude to arrive early to a dinner party. The salt and pepper should always be passed together, and food should always be passed around the table left to right. When using utensils, you should always work from the outside-in. These are all unofficial rules that few people know but many people expect to encounter. Eating has never been so complicated.

Dining Around the World

Americans who travel to other countries are often surprised by some of their common etiquette rules when it comes to dining. In Chile, it's considered rude to eat anything with your hands—even foods like French fries. In France, bread is not to be eaten as appetizer. Additionally, guests should not begin eating until the host or hostess says, "Bon appetite!" If you visit Britain, be sure to always pass a plate of food to the left. Italians only drink cappuccinos before noon, unlike what you generally see in America. Sticking your chopsticks in your rice in Japan is frowned upon and considered to be improper.

Although parmesan cheese is a common topping for Italian food in America, in Italy, you should never ask for parmesan on your food unless it is explicitly given or offered. If you find yourself in Belgium without a bread plate, bread should be placed on the top left rim of your dinner plate. When in Brazil, your hands should always be visible—above the table—unless you are using your utensils. It is also considered rude to cut lettuce up in a salad. In Egypt, and many other parts of Africa and the Middle East, you should not eat with your left hand. When visiting Morocco, you can never place your hands in your mouth, as you'll need to put your hand back in the communal bowl for food.

Scandalous Oreos

Oreo's markets itself as "America's Favorite Cookie", and that's no exaggeration. For years, it has been the bestselling cookie in the country. However, its start was less than stellar. Oreo's cookies were actually created as a knock-off of Hydrox, a sandwich cookie that was introduced to the market in 1908. Unfortunately for Hydrox, their popular sandwich cookies earned a reputation as a copycat of Oreo's cookies several years after Oreo's 1912 launch. Cookie sales saw a decline, and Hydrox would never recover.

GIFs Are Alive and Well

GIFs are more popular than ever, but their roots date back to 1987. Before the internet was what it is today, GIFs—or graphics interchange format—made their way into society as short, silent, usually humorous clips. November 5, 1999, was proclaimed "Burn All

GIFs Day" by a group of people who created a website with the same name. These people wanted to get rid of GIFs, which had saturated the web, and get back to good old-fashioned PNG picture files.

Unfortunately for them, their plan didn't work out so well. Today, GIFs are worth hundreds of millions of dollars. Giphy, the site that allowed Twitter to introduce a library of thousands of GIFs for users, is valued at an estimated $300 million. Imgur is another site that has tried to modernize and switch up GIFs, with a launch of their own GIFV format. Society has begun to use the title of GIF for any video snippet with no sounds, which just goes to show the normalcy of GIFs in everyday life.

On the Lam

Whitey Bulger called Alcatraz Island his home from 1959 to 1963, as a result of armed robbery. Years later, in 1995, Bulger went on the run after learning from a crooked FBI agent that there was likely an indictment for murder and racketeering coming for him. After sixteen years on the lam, he was finally arrested in 2011. He was found guilty on over thirty counts, with his crimes including eleven murders and racketeering.

Criminals going into hiding—and eventually being found— is nothing out of the ordinary. The odd twist in the story comes with one of Bulger's sightseeing adventures. While he was a fugitive, Bulger posed as an ordinary tourist and toured Alcatraz. He even put on a prisoner costume to pose with his girlfriend at the time—a fellow mobster—for a picture on the tour. In the picture, which is believed to have been taken just a few weeks after he fled, he can be seen grinning from ear-to-ear. Talk about hiding in plain sight.

Swedes and Coffee

Coffee in Sweden dates back to the 1670s, and was first a popular beverage amongst the elite. In the mid-1700s, it was banned from the country due in part to the high taxes, and it became a black-market type beverage. Why did King Gustav III want coffee out of his country for good? He worried that coffee caused health problems, and he became paranoid that meetups to drink coffee could result in power-hungry citizens trying to take over the country.

King Gustav III thought that the best way he could possibly get his fellow Swedes to stop drinking coffee was to prove its harm through a science experiment. A set of twins had been sentenced to death, but he offered their freedom in exchange for participation in an experiment. He had one twin drink three cups of tea each day for the remainder of his life, and the other twin drink three cups of coffee. In a twist of irony, King Gustav III was assassinated before he got to witness the results—which didn't make a difference anyway, because the twin who drank coffee outlived the twin who drank tea. They both lived to be more than 83 years old, quite a feat for the time period. More than that, both twins outlived all of the doctors who were in charge of monitoring their health.

The coffee ban was removed once and for all in the 1820s. Today, coffee is an important part of Swedish culture. Swedes often take two breaks for coffee, which they call fika, each day, and Sweden is the country with the third-highest coffee consumption in the world.

Why, Wyoming?

Wyoming isn't as high-tech as some other states in the US, but one thing that surprises many is the lack of escalators. As of 2013, in the entire state of Wyoming only had two escalators, or four, if you count each set. Both escalators are found in the city of Casper—one at the Hilltop National Bank, and one at the First National Bank. If you break down the numbers, that's a miniscule 0.000003467 escalators per capita. When asked why escalators aren't prevalent in Wyoming, officials shared that it was just more cost-effective to not have escalators, and that stairs are safer than elevators in the event of a fire or emergency. Unfortunately, the lack of escalators has also resulted in the lack of education and practice when it comes to escalators. People in Wyoming don't know how to properly maneuver escalators, which has resulted in some serious injuries.

Congress' Bunker

The Greenbrier Bunker was one of America's best-kept secrets for decades. Beneath the Greenbrier Resort in West Virginia, a bomb shelter was hidden from the general public. It was created for members of Congress in the event of an emergency, stocked with months' worth of food and supplies. The bunker was kept a secret for over thirty years, and it was built alongside the Greenbrier Resort, in the town of White Sulphur Springs.

Even the official historian of Greenbrier, Bob Conte, knew nothing about the bunker. Conte had all sorts of records and photos from the property, but nothing that revealed information about the bunker. It turns out that the bunker was built in case of an emergency during the Cold War. The space of the bunker has been compared to that of a Walmart store, with thick, concrete walls and an extensive air filtration system. Rows of metal bunkbeds line the walls, with enough beds for 1,100 people.

The building of the bunker was called "Project Greek Island," and hotel workers and locals were told the construction was for a new conference and exhibition center. It was even used for conferences by thousands of people who had no idea that it was actually designed to be a secret bunker. Down the hall from the sleeping quarters, there was a room designed to be the floor for the House of Representatives. A group of secret government employees disguised themselves as technicians, but they were really some of the only people in the world who knew about the bunker. It was their job to make sure there was a constant six-month supply of food, the most up-to-date pharmaceuticals, and everything that the members of Congress would need in the event of an emergency.

The bunker was exposed to the public in 1992. Today, the Greenbrier property is home to not only the Greenbrier Resort, but also the Presidents' Cottage Museum. As over twenty-five presidents have stayed there, the museum shows their experiences, the property's history, and, now, part of the bunker. There is a new emergency shelter in place, but only a handful of people know its whereabouts.

Is That Chicken in There?

Fast food generally has a bad reputation, and Trent University didn't help one fast food chain's credibility. In early 2017, a researcher at the college, based in Ontario, decided to run a test on Subway's chicken to see if it was, in fact, chicken. The results showed that Subway's chicken strips were made up of only 43% chicken, while their oven-roasted chicken had 54% chicken DNA. The rest of the ingredients were simply filler ingredients. While no one expected fast food chicken to be 100% chicken, no one expected the results to be as low as they were.

Consistent testing showed a pattern—that much of the DNA of the "chicken" was soy protein. Other fast food restaurants, like McDonald's and Tim Horton's, were found to have between 85% and 90% of chicken DNA in their chicken products. Panel testing done amongst consumers supported the results, with all taste testers ranking Subway's chicken amongst their least favorite. They noted that the sample from Subway tasted more artificial than the chicken from other fast food chains. Subway has maintained that their chicken is 100% white meat chicken, with limited artificial ingredients. The test results beg to differ.

The Other Flight

September 11, 2001 is known for four flights, in particular, the two planes that were flown into the World Trade Center, the one that was aimed at the Pentagon, and the one that crashed in Shanksville, Pennsylvania. Air travel was halted until further notice—with the exception of extreme cases.

One of these exceptions was for Kareena, a six-month-old in Houston who was dying of liver failure. Without a liver, her doctors predicted she would be dead within 48 hours. On the same night that the doctors told Kareena's parents about her prognosis, the night of September 10, 2001, an infant passed away in Nashville, Tennessee, eight-hundred miles away from Kareena. The parents of the infant decided to donate her organs, and Kareena's parents were given renewed hope for a donor match for their daughter.

Hours later, news of the terrorist attacks spread in the hospital. With every flight in the entire country grounded, it looked like Kareena wouldn't receive the liver she so greatly needed. Dr. Ravi Chari, the surgeon who was in charge of removing the liver in Nashville, decided that he wouldn't take no for an answer. He had Donor Services get in contact with the Nashville Airport traffic control, to no avail. They were under strict FAA orders not to fly. Then, a woman from the Nashville Tower made a last-ditch effort to get the liver to Kareena. She had her team call the National Guard.

The liver was loaded onto a C-130 with an armed escort, and the Air Guard was, after much back and forth, granted permission to take flight. It was one of the only planes in the sky during the two-hour flight to Houston. Six hours after flight takeoff, Kareena was in the intensive care unit, recovering from the transplant. Dr. Chari said he didn't give up because letting the flight ban prevent them from delivering the liver would have been like letting the terrorists kill someone else.

The Man Behind the Keurig

John Sylvan and Peter Dragone worked together to figure out a better solution for making coffee. In 1992, they founded Keurig, which means "excellence" in

Danish. Sylvan was, after all, the target consumer of the product he was trying to make. In 1995, he went to the hospital after feeling woozy and having heart palpitations. Once a heart attack and brain injury were ruled out, the doctor pursued other avenues of questioning. He finally got to the root of the problem when he asked Sylvan how much coffee he drank on a daily basis. Sylvan's answer? 30 to 40 cups each day. He was diagnosed with caffeine poisoning and told to reduce his coffee intake.

Despite a rough start for the company, coffee became more than just John Sylvan's beverage of choice. It became his life, his livelihood, and his sole focus. It all started in the mid-1980s, when John Sylvan was working in marketing. He felt that the coffee his colleagues drank, along with the system by which they paid, was of poor quality. Coffee sat in the pot for hours, and it became bitter tasting. He knew there had to be a better solution. In the early 1990s, he began trying out different single-serving coffee pod ideas. Once he began prototyping various machines, he brought in Peter Dragone, his former roommate from Colby College, as a 50% partner.

The two men had trouble finding investors and building a machine that was reliable and easy to demonstrate. Once they finally got an investor in 1994, it was a snowball effect. They received over one million dollars in funding, and they were finally able to begin selling commercial brewers. The company took two years to develop an affordable and reliable home model, but it hit store shelves in the mid-2000s. Now, Keurig is worth billions of dollars. Over 13% of all American businesses have Keurig commercial models in the workplace, and at least one out of every four coffee makers sold in the US is Keurig brand. John Sylvan, however, left the company on poor terms, gave up his equity, and received only $50,000. While he wishes he would have considered a royalty deal for the K-cups, or the machines themselves, he says that he's just grateful to have been a part of creating an iconic brand.

Human Centipede 2

One high school teacher in Tennessee made headlines in 2016 for an unusual reason: they decided to show *Human Centipede 2 (Full Sequence)* to their class of high school students. The film is centered on a man who kidnaps people and sews them together—from mouth to anus—and wasn't even allowed in theaters in the United Kingdom due to how gruesome it was. It took 32 cuts from the movie for the British Board of Film Classification to allow it to be shown in theaters.

The seemingly naïve director of the film franchise, Tom Six, went on Twitter to share his support of the teacher, saying that it should be a mandatory film for students to see, due its supposed focus on bullying. Parents, on the other hand, were outraged, having not been notified of the film showing ahead of time, and the teacher was ultimately suspended. The teacher's reason for showing the movie? To this day, no one truly knows.

A Salary Poorly Capped

Doormen in New York City live on small salaries, and the poor tips they receive don't help. One story has continued to be passed down through a group of doormen at a high-end building on Park Avenue. There is a wealthy doctor who lives in the building that keeps a spreadsheet of how long each doorman has been employed. His reason? Their holiday tip depends on how long they have been there. If a doorman has been there for one year, they get $1. If they've been there for 20 years, they get $20. The amount of work a doorman does for his family has no bearing on how much he receives as a holiday gift.

This is just one story of an even bigger web. It is said that the rich areas of New York City have the worst tippers, especially when it comes to doormen. The salary cap for a unionized doorman in New York City is $44,000 each year, which is meager means for someone who lives in, or commutes to, one of the most expensive cities to live in in the country. While $44,000 may seem difficult enough to live on in New York City, the average doorman makes around $30,000 per year. Some of the people living in these buildings have a net worth into the billions of dollars, but most doormen get a mere $15 around the holidays.

A prime example of this is David Koch. David Koch is number 4 on the Forbes 400. An oil mogul, he has an estimated net worth of $36 billion. Koch is also known for not tipping the doormen at his residence on Park Avenue. Despite loading up his cars for weekly trips to the Hamptons, doormen have not received a tip—or even a smile—from Koch. They consider themselves lucky if they get a $50 check around Christmastime.

The Ticket Tricker

Aktarer Zaman was just 22-years-old when he founded a website in 2014. He had no clue it would lead to a lawsuit and angering some well-established companies. His crime? Being clever. Zaman started Skiplagged as a way to help people find cheaper flights through a method he calls "hidden city ticketing". The premise is simple: you can buy a ticket on a flight that has a layover in your actual destination, and only travel the first leg of the flight you have booked.

For example, if you want to visit Dallas from your home of Boston, you could book a flight from Boston to Los Angeles with a layover in Dallas, then get off in Dallas and never take the last leg of the itinerary. Of course, this only works if you are not checking bags, but it has helped thousands of people find cheaper flight options. United and Orbitz, who have a combined worth of billions, sued Aktarer Zaman, saying that Skiplagged promoted prohibited travel practices and provided unfair competition.

They sued for $75,000, which they said was lost revenue. At the time of the lawsuit, Zaman was making no profit, stating that he was simply trying to help travelers find the best deals. Nowadays, if you visit Skiplagged's website, you'll find an interesting tagline. It reads, "We're better at finding cheap flights than anyone else—so good, United Airlines actually sued us for it."

America's Favorite Beverage

After a fifteen-year break, water reemerged as the most popular drink in the United States in 2013. Soda was the most widely-consumed beverage for over two decades leading up to 1998, its peak year. Americans were consuming a whopping 54 gallons of soda per person, per year, compared to just 42 gallons of water. Every five to ten years, the tables turn, and soda and water switch places in popularity. Many people attribute the increase of water's popularity to the rising obesity rates and increased interest in healthy eating and dieting. Americans average 44 gallons of soda a year, which is a 17% decrease from its peak, while water has increased 38% to 58 gallons a year.

Never Too Late

It is customary for Jewish boys and girls to celebrate their bar and bat mitzvah, generally at the age of thirteen—or twelve in some denominations. This is the ceremony that welcomes them into Jewish adulthood, and it is something Jewish children grow up looking forward to. For Yisrael Kristal, his big day took a bit longer than he thought. Now recognized as the world's oldest man, Kristal was born in 1903 in Poland. His original bar mitzvah was canceled while his father fought in the Russian Army in World War I. His mother had passed away three years earlier.

During the Holocaust, Kristal endured the horrors of Auschwitz and lost his wife, two children, and other family members. He moved to Haifa, Israel, where he remarried and worked for many years as a candy maker. At 113 years old, Yisrael Kristal finally got to live out his dream of having a bar mitzvah in September 2016. Nearly 100 family members came from all over to celebrate his special day.

From Willie to Willie

It's no secret that country icon Willie Nelson has had his share of troubles. In 1990, he was hit with a bill for nearly $17 million in unpaid taxes. As a result, he had to get rid of many of his most prized possessions in order to avoid legal ramifications. Fans of Nelson went to auctions and purchased some of his belongings, only to send them back to him. Of course, some fans kept their purchases as their very own piece of Willie, but many returned them to who they felt was their rightful owner. As a way of turning the situation into a joke of sorts, he released an album called *The IRS Tapes: Who Will Buy My Memories?* It seems his fans took him literally.

Indy 500

The Indianapolis 500 has been around for over a century, with the first race taking place in 1911. The tradition is that thirty-three cars compete in the Indy 500, which takes its name from the 500-mile distance of the race. It was the first 500-mile car race by almost fifty years, and it is considered to be the most famous auto race in the world. Upon finishing the race, it is tradition that the winner of the Indy 500 pulls into Victory Lane and takes a sip of milk.

Based on the average speed the racecar drivers travel, they are able to cover the distance of a football field in less than a single second. The average pit stop, for adjustments, fuel, and wheel changes, takes approximately fifteen seconds. The Indianapolis Motor Speedway, where it takes place each year, is not actually in Indianapolis. It's in its own town called Speedway, Indiana, which has a population of around 12,000. The town of Speedway has its own town government, police force, and schools.

Female Directors

Hollywood has come a long way when it comes to allowing women to play a role in the film industry, but some feats have still been primarily kept by men.

Niki Caro, director of films like *The Zookeeper's Wife* and *Whale Rider*, was chosen in early 2017 to be the director of a live-action version of Disney's *Mulan*. This makes her just the fourth woman in Hollywood history to be the sole director of a live-action movie with a budget exceeding $100 million. Two of the other women have directed upcoming releases, while Kathryn Bigelow directed *K-19: The Widowmaker* over a decade ago.

Caro is the fifth woman to direct any film—not just live-action—with a budget over $100 million. Jennifer Yuh Nelson directed *Kung Fu Panda 2* but was later given a male co-director for the third installment of the franchise. Controversy has been brewing in recent years over the lack of female directors, especially due to the hiring of younger, less qualified male directors for huge undertakings. Disney has expressed interest in searching for female directors for several upcoming films in the coming years.

A Man and His Statue

Some people just take being vain to the next level. The president of Turkmenistan, President Gurbanguly Berdymukhamedov, decided that the country needed more of him—so he had a giant statue of himself built in the center of the capital city. The statue is comprised of a cliff made of white marble, with the president depicted riding a golden horse. It sits in downtown Ashgabat and was revealed in 2015. President Berdymukhamedov's reasoning for having the statue be built? He says it's what the people were asking for. The president maintains that the people of Turkmenistan put together a proposal to honor him with a statue in honor of over a decade as president.

The statue, which stands at a whopping 69-feet, is reminiscent of the Bronze Horsemen statue that honors Peter the Great in St. Petersburg. It joins several other massive tributes to world leaders, one of which is in the same country. Saparmurat Niazov, the president of Turkmenistan before Berdymukhamedov, had a golden statue built of himself years earlier. When Berdymukhamedov came to power after Niazov's death, he immediately had the golden statue moved to the edge of Ashgabat.

Translation of a Nation

Jimmy Carter accomplished a lot as the 39th president of the United States, but most people don't realize the impact he had on translation and language relations. The televised event during which President Carter officially accepted his nomination as the Democratic candidate was the first time a sign language interpreter appeared on a nationally televised event. At Carter's inauguration parade, he recognized members of the Navajo Code Talkers. This was important not only to acknowledge the cultural differences in the country, but also to show appreciation for their service in World War II and recognize that the war could have had a much different outcome without their help.

President Carter quickly learned the impact language barriers could have when he had his own speech mishap. While in Poland to give a speech, he had a line that included, "My desires for the Polish people." The interpreter, who hadn't seen a copy of the speech beforehand, translated that as, "My lusts for the Polish people." It was interpreted in a way that had a more sexual connotation, and was quite embarrassing for the president. From that point forward, President Carter had his speechwriters consulting with interpreters, and he even delivered parts of speeches in other languages.

Under President Carter, the Court Interpreters Act was put into effect in October 1978. This would allow any person with limited English knowledge to have a court interpreter with them. Shortly after, he signed the Disabilities Act of 1978, which was later amended into the Americans with Disabilities Act. This law allowed the deaf community more access to interpreters.

Snacks for Sale

Kids are suspended from school for all sorts of reasons—fighting, talking back to a teacher, breaking the dress code. One boy in Italy made headlines in 2016 for a much simpler reason—he was suspended for selling snack foods at school. The boy, who was a 17-year-old student in Turin, would take orders from friends and fellow students for snacks and sodas, then buy them at a convenience store and sell them for a cheaper price than the school cafeteria. When the school found out about it the first time, a year earlier, the student was suspended for ten days.

Once they found out he had started up his snack business a second time, they increased his suspension to fifteen days. The media caught wind of the situation, and debate ensued. Some people felt the school was right to suspend him, while others felt that the school was dampening his entrepreneurial abilities. He was even offered jobs from various startups, as well as a scholarship from an institute that said that the boy's initiative should be celebrated, not punished.

Cool as A Cucumber

President Calvin Coolidge was known as "Silent Cal", for his quiet demeanor. However, for those in the White House, he was also known for his childish behavior and practical jokes. He would also often nap during the day and leave early from state dinners. One of his favorite pranks to play was calling for his bodyguards then hiding underneath his desk while they searched for him. He let them presume he had been kidnapped and would let them frantically look for him.

Buzz About the Bentley

In 2013, Chiquinho Scarpa, a wealthy businessman from Brazil, made a startling announcement on his Facebook page: he planned to bury his Bentley Continental Flying Spur underground. The reasoning he gave was that he wanted to be able to drive the car, worth $400,000, in the afterlife. He shared photos of his progress as he dug the hole in his backyard, which sent social media into a frenzy. People wondered how he could bury something so valuable when it could be sold or donated to charity. They called him crazy and selfish.

The outrage turned to intrigue when Scarpa revealed that the entire announcement was a publicity stunt. The cause? Organ donation. It was National Organ Donation Week in Brazil. He shared a new photo on his Facebook page several days after the initial post, with a banner behind him reading, "It's absurd to bury something much more valuable than a Bentley: your organs." Scarpa shared that he had not, in fact, buried his car, but that the post was intended to get people talking and show how valuable different things can be to different people.

A Remarkable Double Life

After studying medicine at University of Edinburgh, James Barry made a name for himself as a top army surgeon in the early to mid-1800s. He worked all over the world, from Cape Town, South Africa, to

Trinidad and Tobago. Barry was known as a bad-tempered, eccentric person by his colleagues, and he was often teased until he shot one of his tormentors dead. Despite the common dislike of Barry, he was a well-liked doctor and ended his career as Inspector General of military hospitals.

James Barry died of a severe stomach illness in 1865. That's when the mystery began to unfold. As his maid prepared him for the funeral, she made the startling discovery that he was actually a woman. Some colleagues maintained that they knew Barry's true identity all along, while most were shocked by the revelation. James Barry was born Margaret Ann Bulkley in Ireland. She planned to disguise herself as a man to study medicine in Edinburgh, then travel to Venezuela to practice medicine as a woman. With a letter of recommendation in hand from the prestigious Lord Buchan, Margaret and her mother took a boat to Leith, near Edinburgh, and organized her disguise. Margaret's plans were interrupted when General Francisco de Miranda, to whom her family had ties, failed in his attempt to liberate Venezuela. Margaret decided to continue in her disguise as James Barry and join the army, where she spent the rest of her life as James Barry.

D.R. McKinnon was Barry's doctor and the one who ultimately wrote "male" on the death certificate. When asked if he knew the truth about Barry's gender, McKinnon said that he never had any suspicion that Dr. Barry was female, but that it wasn't his business either way. Shortly after his death, a woman who worked at the hospital performed the last offices—to confirm that Barry was dead—and said that she believed he was actually a female and had marks that indicated she had given birth at a young age. No information has ever been found about a possible child of Margaret Ann Bulkley. Over a century later, it is still unknown whether Margaret changed her gender identity and considered herself to be a man, or if she was simply undercover for all those years.

Kung Fu Success

Kung Fu Panda was not only successful because it was a hit at the box office. It was also deemed to be an accurate depiction of Chinese architecture, myths, and culture that was done extremely well. The film upset many top filmmakers in China, but not because it was offensive. They wished that they had made the movie about their own country. Viewers from all over the world were impressed that, despite the film being a comedic cartoon, they were able to accurately portray the ideas of family expectations and the afterlife, as well as the martial arts scenes.

Filmmakers have said that they didn't think Western countries would be interested in movies about their traditional culture, while others say a movie of that means was simply too expensive to be made in China. *Kung Fu Panda* cost over $130 million to produce, while most movies produced in China cap out around $1.5 million. They also don't have the same level of animation that can be found in Hollywood. Many ordinary citizens in China say that people in China are often so busy trying to keep up with the latest Western trends that they tend to overlook their own appeal and culture. Top Chinese actors and producers hold out hope that China can produce a film of this caliber someday.

War and Poop

During the Civil War, both sides saw a massive problem: diarrhea. The Confederacy was lacking in food supply, while the Union had plenty of food—with the exception of the siege in Chattanooga— but saw the effects of nutritional deficiency. Throughout the US Civil War, there were twice as many deaths due to disease, such as malnutrition and dysentery, as there were deaths due to injuries on the battlefield. This was often due to spoiled foods or foods that were prepared improperly. One of the most unique codes of honor during the war? There came to be a mutual understanding amongst soldiers that you could not shoot at someone while they were in the midst of having a bowel movement.

The Story Behind the Legend

Before the *Indiana Jones* franchise was known around the world, it was simply an idea—thought up by a guy who was on top of the world. It was shortly after the premiere of George Lucas' first *Star Wars* movie in 1977, and he was brainstorming new project ideas. He met up with a longtime friend of his, who just happened to be Steven Spielberg. Spielberg revealed that he really wanted to direct a James Bond film, and had even gone to the owners of the *James Bond* series to ask about directing, but they turned him down.

Lucas had other plans. He told Spielberg that he had a story in mind that was like James Bond, but better. It was the story of an archeologist, named Indiana Smith, after Lucas' dog, Indiana. Steven Spielberg hated the name and wanted to change it to something else that didn't sound quite so corny. George Lucas' response? "Name him Indiana Jones, or whatever you want! It's your movie now." *Raiders of the Lost Ark*, the first Indiana Jones Film, went on to win four Oscars and accrue over a dozen award nominations.

All the Crimes

Who says criminals don't have morals? In August 2008, several men broke into a house in North Yorkshire, England. Amongst the items they stole was a laptop, on which they soon found images that they suspected were child pornography. The criminals turned themselves in and brought the laptop to the police, which led to the conviction of Richard Coverdale. Coverdale had 78 illegal files—65 movies, and 13 images—on the computer. He admitted to talking to a 14-year-old girl in an online chatroom and was sentences to three and a half years in jail. The detective on the case praised the burglars for having a conscience and turning in Richard Coverdale.

A Crazy Settlement

Herb Sukenik was a 73-year-old recluse living in the Mayflower Hotel when it was purchased by developers in 2004. Part of the job of the Zeckendorfs, the brothers who had purchased the property and several adjacent lots, was to buy out or relocate the residents of the top floors of the apartments. The leases of these tenants prevented them from being evicted, and their apartments had been rent-controlled for decades. There were four old men left.

One man was 98 years old and went to live with family in Mexico, taking a $1 million check from the Zeckendorfs with him. Two other men lived in their own apartments and were given similar checks in exchange for vacating their apartments. Finally, the Zeckendorfs got to Herb Sukenik. Herb, who held a master's, Ph.D., and M.D. and never married, had lived in the building for nearly thirty years. His apartment was away from the rest of them, and he lived in seclusion, too intelligent to connect with others.

Sukenik refused the money. During his three

decades at the Mayflower Hotel, he had spent most of his time in his tiny room. He was not well-liked by the staff or his fellow residents. Despite being entitled to maid service, he let the mold accumulate in his apartment and spent his days doing crossword puzzles in silence. He had worked as a school doctor from time to time, but he eventually retreated from society and spent his days in his apartment. The Zeckendorfs turned to their relocation attorney to help reach a deal with Sukenik.

The attorney engaged in negotiations with Sukenik, who did research into the acreage of the property, what the Zeckendorfs had paid, and what properties were worth at that point in time. His demand was simple, in his eyes: he wanted a new apartment with a view of the park. Sukenik found the rental of his dreams—2,200 square feet, two bedrooms, and right on Central Park South. He tried to add in other demands to the deal, like free meals twice a week at an acclaimed restaurant, but the Zeckendorfs refused.

Once the Zeckendorfs had purchased the condo for Sukenik to live in, he decided he wanted money, as well, despite having no need for it. The Zeckendorfs resisted and began construction on one half of the property. Sukenik maintained that the construction noise didn't bother him, and that he actually liked listening to the noise. Finally, the Zeckendorfs caved. In addition to paying $2 million for the condo Sukenik wanted to live in, they paid him an additional sum, estimated at $17 million. It became the most expensive price ever paid to relocate one tenant in New York City.

They're Just Puppets

Sesame Street celebrated its 40th anniversary back in 2009 by giving the spotlight to each Muppet for a day. One of the main focuses? Bert and Ernie's relationship. For decades, viewers have debated the sexuality of the characters, who they feel seem to be more than just friends. Pop culture has fed into this rumor, with spoofs like "Ernest & Bertram" and allusions in shows, like in Avenue Q. It got to the point where, in the early 1990s, the show's producers put out an announcement stating that the characters did not portray a gay couple and that they have no plans for them to do so. The main point they tried to get across? Bert and Ernie are just puppets.

What the Webcam?

With great technology comes great responsibility — or at least that's what some of the most notable people in the world are thinking. Mark Zuckerberg revealed in a photo that he tapes over his webcam and microphone jack on his laptop. Similarly, James Comey, former FBI director, puts a piece of tape over the camera. Though they haven't been clear about their reasoning — with the exception of Comey alluding to copying Zuckerberg with the idea — it seems to be for fear of hackers and privacy breaches. Both have not given any specific data or research to back up their reasoning. However, many experts have also begun to cover up their webcams, hoping that it will reduce any damage that could occur as a result of a hack.

Half Marathon Hound

The Elkmont Half Marathon takes place in Alabama each year in January. In 2016, the runners had a very special guest join them. Ludivine is a bloodhound who lived near the start of the half marathon route. When the owners let her outside to go to the bathroom, she joined the group of people and began the race alongside them. Ludivine's owner didn't know she was missing—or that she had joined the race—until a friend of hers called to tell her. Despite stopping to play in the water and follow some animals, the hound finished the race in seventh place. As the top-finishing female, Ludivine received a medal. The best part, in the eyes of the race director? The dog had never been on a run with her owner or gone on walks even remotely close to 13.1 miles in length, and she ran the entire thing without a leash or her owner.

Contamination or Not?

Dr. Karl Kruszelnicki ran a science-focused radio show in the early 2000s, which led to one of his most unique experiments ever. A nurse called in wanting to know if she was contaminating the sterile room she worked in when she silently farted. Curious about the answer, Dr. Kruszelnicki vowed to find out. He worked with a microbiologist in Canberra, Australia to devise an experiment. He had a colleague fart directly onto two Petri dishes from a distance of 2 inches away. The first time, he broke wind fully clothed, and, the second time, the doctor had him take his pants down.

They let the Petri dishes sit overnight before analyzing the results. They found that the second Petri dish had grown two lumps of bacteria that are usually only found on the skin or in the gut. The first Petri dish showed nothing, which led Dr. Kruszelnicki to believe that the clothing acted as a barrier or filter. Their final deduction? The bacteria that had come from the second fart was skin bacteria from the butt cheeks, meaning that germs were only being passed when people farted without clothing on. However, he noted that the bacteria were in no way harmful, and that they were actually similar to bacteria found in yogurt.

Good Will Tricking

Before it was an Oscar and Golden Globe winner, *Good Will Hunting* was a script for a modest-budget film written by Matt Damon and Ben Affleck. The two had sent the script to numerous studios, several of which had made them offers. Studios were jumping at the chance to have Matt Damon and Ben Affleck in one of their movies. They ultimately decided to go with Miramax, under the direction of Harvey Weinstein. Their reason? While many made offers, Harvey Weinstein picked up on something that no other producer did. He said he loved the script but had one question: Why was there a sex scene between the two leads—who were both straight men with no romantic feelings for one another—on page 60 of the script? Affleck and Damon shared that they had written this absurd, far-fetched scene to see if the producers they were sending the scripts to actually took the time to read their script. Harvey Weinstein was the only one who mentioned it, so his company was the one that got to produce the movie.

Making Ways Up the Ranks

Julia Stewart became the CEO of Applebee's in 2008, after IHOP purchased Applebee's. It was truly a full-circle experience for Stewart. Then 52 years old at the time of her appointment as CEO, she had started within the company at just 16 years of age. She worked at IHOP as a waitress, beginning in her high school days, and she says she fell in love with the company and the restaurant business. She poured the coffee, wore an apron, and delivered food to the tables. After leaving to attend college and work in restaurant marketing, Stewart returned to IHOP in 2001. During her years away from IHOP and

Applebee's, she even worked as a night shift assistant manager at Taco Bell to make ends meet while staying in the industry. She finally came back as CEO of IHOP, after Applebee's turned her down for a promotion, then she got the chance to take over her former company. Julia Stewart's story is a true Cinderella story—from serving food, to earning a spot on *Forbes'* list of 50 Most Powerful Women in 2007.

Burn, Baby, Burn

Michael Jackson was filming a Pepsi commercial in front of hundreds of fans in 1983, when his hair caught on fire. It was the result of failed pyrotechnics. Jackson, unaware that his hair was burning, continued to dance, until someone ran on stage and put out the fire. In the weeks that followed, he had horrible migraines until the burns finally healed. Many thought that Michael Jackson would sue Pepsi as a result of the trauma he endured, but he had a much different idea. He settled out of court with them, and used the money to build a burn center at the medical center in Culver City, California, he was treated at. The Michael Jackson Burn Center at Brotman Medical Center remained open for several years, until it was shut down as a result of decreased funding from the government.

Millions to Many

Harris Rosen was fired from his job at Disney World in the early 1970s because despite playing a role in the development of resorts including the Contemporary and Polynesian, they didn't feel he was a "company man". Upon his firing, he used his life savings to put a deposit down on a Quality Inn, where his office remains to this day. He has now spent decades in the hospitality industry, designing buildings and building one of the largest hotel groups in Florida from the ground up. Rosen Hotels & Resorts now has seven properties in the Orlando area—but Rosen didn't let that go to his head.

In 1993, Rosen went into a high-poverty, drug-ridden area of Orlando called Tangelo Park and created the Tangelo Park Program. It provided every two to four-year-old child in the neighborhood with free preschool and a free college education for every student who graduated from high school. The graduation rate amongst Tangelo Park increased to 100%, and students who went to schools in the state of Florida had all of their tuition and living expenses covered. But Rosen's good deeds didn't stop there. He pledged 20 acres of property from one of his resorts and $10 million to build a new school as part of UCF. The Rosen College of Hospitality Management opened in 2004, and, if it had been up to Rosen, it would have been built on the helms of an anonymous donor without his name attached to the building. Millions of dollars later, and Rosen is still working out of the small office the first hotel he ever purchased.

The Freshest Sandwich

When Andy George uploaded a video on YouTube in 2015, entitled "How to Make a $1500 Sandwich in Only Six Months," everyone thought it was a joke. What they didn't know was that George really had taken on the task of creating every aspect of a sandwich completely from scratch as part of a new web series he was creating. He started by growing a garden of his own vegetables and even took a flight to the West Coast to make salt when he found it was impossible to do in his home state of Minnesota without accessible mines. George had to build his own press in order to extract oil from the sunflowers he had grown. He even went so far as to harvest his own wheat, milk a cow to make cheese, and slaughter a chicken.

If that wasn't enough, he also collected honey—bees and all—and made his own butter from scratch. In total, it took George six months to have everything ready, and it cost him $1,500. Once his task was complete, he invited his friends over for a taste-test. The verdict was that his homegrown vegetables tasted better than the ones bought at the store, but that the sandwich made with store-bought ingredients was better overall. George's response to the sandwich he spent six months making? "It's not bad."

Brace Face

Like most kids, Amos Dudley has braces as a teenager. But, as he got older, he felt his teeth starting to shift back, and he began to get more self-conscious about his smile. At 24 years old, the New Jersey Institute of Technology (NJIT) student set out to find his own solution. After all, what college student can afford the thousands of dollars companies like Invisalign and Damon charge for clear braces? Dudley used equipment at NJIT to scan models of his teeth then printed them out and molded plastic—non-toxic, of course—around them. The most difficult part for Dudley was the research. He had to figure out the correct measurements to realign his teeth in order to perfect the design and prevent damage to his teeth. Finally, he used a 3D printer at the school to create the alignment trays. With four months of use, Dudley's teeth made noticeable improvements. The best part? It cost him a mere $60 total, all for the materials.

Beginnings in Disney

When Walt Disney began plans for Walt Disney World, he decided to keep it as much of a secret as he could. Before deciding on a location, he and his team searched for years for a site. They considered opening a theme park in New Jersey, but passed due to the seasonality they would have due to weather. They looked at areas all over the world, almost deciding on St. Louis, until they finally decided on Florida. As the project began taking formation, it was given the title of "Project X".

Everyone hired on the project needed to remain top-secret, and Disney used fake company names when making land purchases so that no one would figure out what he was doing. Some of the dummy companies he created? Retlaw ("Walter" written backwards), Bay Lake Properties, and M.T. Lott Real Estate. Even the Florida government was kept out of the loop. Locals began to speculate as to who was purchasing these large plots of land. By the time a reporter caught on to Walt Disney, he had already purchased 27,000 acres of land in swampy areas across two Florida counties. On November 15, 1965, the official announcement was made about the building of the new Disney park.

Drone Conclusions

Wachipan is an indigenous community in the southern region of Guyana. Residents of the area are consistently worried about threats of the forest destruction in their community, so several members of the community decided to take matters into their own hands. Simply by watching tutorial videos on YouTube, they created a fixed-wing model drone with a camera mounted atop. The purpose of the drone was to capture images and videos of illegal logging to bring to the government, as the government would not intervene without proof.

YouTube saves the day!

Math Genius

Greg Bernard Dantzig was a doctorate student at the University of California, Berkley, in 1939. He walked in late to his statistics class one day, saw two problems written on the board, and wrote them down in his notebook to do for homework. What Dantzig didn't know was that these were not, in fact, homework problems, but examples of famous unsolved statistics problems. He took them home and unknowingly solved them. Dantzig noted that he turned his homework several days late, but apologized to the professor, explaining that he felt the problems were difficult than what they were learning. The homework paper was left to join a pile of papers on the professor's desk.

Weeks later, his professor came to him and told him that one of his answers was going to be published. Dantzig, of course, had no clue what the professor was referring to until he explained the mix-up. When it came time for Dantzig to do his thesis, the professor told him to simply put together the binder with the two problems, and that would be acceptable as his thesis. Nearly a decade after his initial finding, Dantzig was given the distinction of co-author for the second problem, when a mathematician reached the same solution that he had.

A Little Humor

Good Humor is best known for their ice cream bars, such as the strawberry shortcake and toasted almond, but their story goes back nearly a century. Harry Burt created the ice cream after his daughter was complaining that one of his ice cream creations was delicious but too messy. In order to secure the patent, Burt went to the patent office with a bucket of Good Humor bars for officials to taste. He was granted the patent in 1923, and the first Good Humor plant was opened in 1929.

One of the most popular traditions of the early Good Humor days was the requirement of Good Humor men to salute men and tip their hats to women. In order to become a Good Humor man, it required three days of orientations and training. A comedic crime film, *The Good Humor Man,* brought more attention to the ice cream upon its release in 1950, centering on a Good Humor ice cream truck driver. Harry Burt initially chose the name Good Humor for the brand, as he felt that there was a correlation between someone's "humor" and their sense of taste. In his mind, "Good Humor" meant great sense of taste and a tasty product.

The Role That Almost Was

Britney Spears has worn a variety of hats, from touring pop star, to star of the low-rated film, *Crossroads*. However, the one role that Britney *didn't* follow through with is the one that made all of the headlines. In 2009, Spears was considering taking part in a movie about the Holocaust, called "The Yellow Star of Sophia and Eton." She would have played a girl who travels back in time to Germany and falls in love with a boy in a concentration camp. The Central Council of Jews in Germany released a statement proclaiming their disgust with the film idea and the potential of Spears being cast in the role. The president of the Central Council said that she believed the only reason they wanted to attach a star of her caliber to the film was to get funding, and that they should have more heavily weighed ethical considerations. The movie faded into obscurity, with no casting or filming ever taking place.

An Accent No More

Born in London, England, Gary Oldman is known for films like *Sid and Nancy, The Dark Knight,* and the *Harry Potter* series. Oldman has been acting since he was a child and made his United States breakthrough in 1991. In fact, he has lived in the United States for such a long time that he had to hire voice coach in order to keep and relearn his British accent. Oldman needed his full-fledged British accent—as opposed to the American one he had acquired—for his role as an intelligence officer in *Tinker Tailor Spy Soldier* in 2011. As such, he invested in a dialect tutor to make sure his accent remained as authentic as the day he left England.

Who's in the Wrong?

In 2013, charges were brought against a female police officer, Laurie Gillespie, in Battle Creek, Michigan, for theft. Department leaders told Gillespie that video footage had caught her searching through other officers' coats and stealing money from one officer's pocket. The twist? The video had been filmed in the women's locker room. When a meeting was held with various higher-ups, Officer Gillespie, and her union representative, the video of the theft was shown. Footage showed female officers dressing and undressing, and it brought up the question of whether or not this was an invasion of privacy. In return, Gillespie and three other female officers sued the city and the police department. An unknown settlement was reached out of court, but the department maintained that they had spoken to legal counsel before installing cameras and had been told it would be all right as long as a female put the cameras there.

Freezing Fat

Using cold to freeze off fat has become an increasingly popular method over the past decade. But does it actually work? Scientists say yes. People have two different types of fat tissue—white fat and brown fat. White fat is the fat that has the appearance of "chub", that people work to get rid of. Brown fat, however, is used to generate body heat. Freezing the white fat can turn it into a cross between the two types of fat, which scientists have begun to call "beige". They say that simply placing an ice pack onto a fatty area of the body can help burn away some of the fat, by beginning the process of transitioning white fat to "beige" fat. A study done by scientists at the University of Kentucky School of Medicine found that tissue samples taken from fat tissue in the winter had more "beige" fat, supporting the idea that the cold helps get rid of this kind of fat.

Stepbrothers for Life

Stepbrothers is a favorite modern comedy, but not without its quirks. For starters, the original version of the movie was nearly five hours long. After a great deal of editing, they cut it down to the 98-minute version that has been seen worldwide. The idea for the film came about when John C. Reilly and Will Ferrell met up with director Adam McKay during the editing for *Talladega Nights*. Some ideas were passed around, but the following day, someone said "bunk beds" and it struck McKay with the core idea for the film.

One of the most difficult aspects for the costume designer was finding older clothes for Ferrell and Reilly to wear without it seeming like their characters were trying to dress as hipsters. As a result, Susan Matheson, the costume designer, made Brennan's Star Wars pajama pants out of bedsheets she purchased online. Will Ferrell's favorite keepsake from set—and the only one he took home with him— is Brennan's prosthetic testicles. Made by one of the most sought-after Hollywood effects companies, they cost a whopping $10,000 to make.

Fans may remember NFL analyst Cris Collinsworth's cameo in the film. While playing Brennan's boss, he refused to say any lines with profanity. Each time he was given a new line with a curse word in it, he would change it up without the curse. Another celebrity appearance was Pablo Cruise. A T-shirt with the band's name was worn by one of the characters in the movie trailer. The band members were so excited that they arranged to perform at the movie's premiere.

First Phrases

In addition to having an undeniable impact on America's history, many presidents have also had the distinction of creating or popularizing common words and phrases that are still used today. George Washington was the first to use the term "administration" as it is currently used in politics. He is also cited with having the first written usage of over thirty words, from "indoors" to "average". Thomas Jefferson also had his fair share of contributions to the modern English language. He introduced words like "mammoth" and "belittle" to common usage, and he also came up with the word "pedicure" as a way to describe the care and treatment of feet and toenails.

Today, we know the group of men who wrote the Constitution and Declaration of Independence as the Founding Fathers. That term came to be by President Warren G. Harding, when he was a senator representing Ohio. Harding was simply known for using alliteration, which solidified the term for him during his presidential campaign. People had previously referred to the group of men as "framers". Similarly, before Zachary Taylor, the wife of the president was usually referred to as a "presidentress". When writing a eulogy for Dolley Madison, Taylor used the term "First Lady". It caught on and became the eventual official term when referring to the president's wife.

Hot Potato

Potatoes were first introduced to Europe from the Americas in the late 1500s and early 1600s. While the government was thrilled with this crop that could grow in years that other crops failed, and grow much more quickly than wheat crops, the general public was much less enthused. Some priests and other clergy members claimed that God had not meant for people to consume potatoes. Herbalists felt that the appearance of the potato plant suggested that it could cause leprosy. People began to believe that potatoes were poisonous, to the point where the plant was associated with worshipping the devil and practicing witchcraft.

It wasn't until war struck Europe in the 1700s that

people turned to potatoes for nourishment. It gave them an opportunity to learn that potatoes, of course, did not cause infection or bring about the practice of witchcraft. By the late 1700s, potatoes were being planted everywhere, and leaders like Frederick the Great in Prussia and Catherine the Great in Russia were encouraging the cultivation of potato plants. Catherine the Great even believed that potatoes could serve as an antidote to famishment.

When a scientist from France, Antoine-Augustin Parmentier, spent three years in a jail in Prussia, his entire diet consisted solely of potatoes. He went back to his country upon his release and wrote an essay about the merits of the potato, and he was able to convince other scientists of their value. To take it a step further, Parmentier organized a birthday banquet for the king, with potato dishes being served, and convinced Marie Antoinette, the king's wife, to wear potato flowers in her hair. These drastic measures finally convinced the general public that potatoes were safe to eat and a valuable crop to grow.

Finger Lickin' Good

It seems someone in Hong Kong wanted to cash in on the success Kentucky Fried Chicken (KFC) has had in the United States. In 2016, KFC in Hong Kong released a new innovation: edible nail polish. The nail polishes came in a several of colors and flavors, like a neutral color for original fried chicken, and burnt orange for hot and spicy. The bottles even had KFC's famous tagline, "It's Finger Lickin' Good", written on them. The nail polishes were made of edible ingredients, like spice blends and vegetable gum, and had to be refrigerated. Even refrigerated, the polishes only lasted for five days. KFC Hong Kong worked hard to promote the nail polish, which, if nothing else, got its fair share of publicity and intrigue.

Separated at Birth

Paula Bernstein and Elyse Schein were twins adopted out to separate families, and didn't meet one another until they were 35 years old. What they didn't know is that they were part of a research project that separated identical twins in the 1960s and 1970s in order to see the impact of nature versus nurture. In 2004, Schein contacted the adoption agency that had been in charge of her case in order to find out more about her birth mom. Instead, she found out that she had a twin sister. The parents did not know that their adopted children had an identical twin, or that the subject of the study was separation of identical twins. They had simply been told that their children were, upon their adoption, already part of a child study that was ongoing through childhood.

Peter Neubauer and Viola Bernard, who specialized in child psychology and consulted with the agency from which the twins were adopted, began the study in the late 1960s. Bernard felt that twins being raised in the same environment—including being dressed similarly and treated the exact same—hindered their development. A year after the study ended, in 1981, a law was created in New York, the state from which Paula and Elyse were adopted, that required adoption agencies to keep all siblings together.

Neubauer later stated that he had no remorse for separating the twins. At the time, it was believed that it was better for twins to be separated at birth and raised independently. Paula and Elyse found that they had a lot of the same interests and personality traits despite being raised in separate households. They even wrote a book, *Identical Strangers*, as a way of explaining and trying to understand what happened to them. The most astonishing part? Neubauer shared that, while one set of triplets and two other sets of twins in the study had found one another, four remaining test subjects still did not know that they had a twin.

White House Chefs

Chefs for the President of the United States each come with their own unique story. In the early days, many of the White House chefs were slaves. Besides the Roman hero, Hercules—and the Disney film adaptation of the mythological figure—there is another notable Hercules. Hercules was one of George Washington's slaves and his personal chef at Mt. Vernon. A portrait found of Hercules piqued curiosity in regard to the slaves of the most famous early political figures in America. Washington's cook followed him to Philadelphia, the nation's capital at the time, and was known for wearing a white chef's outfit and kerchief at all times. It is rumored that Martha Washington was the one who taught Hercules how to cook. He oversaw eight staff members, from waiters to stewards. Eventually, Hercules escaped on the streets of Philadelphia, never to be seen again.

James Hemings was the slave chef for Thomas Jefferson on Monticello. When Jefferson was appointed to the role of minister to France, he brought Hemings with him to learn the art of French cooking. He served as Jefferson's chef for several years before petitioning for his freedom. Jefferson agreed, so long as James would train someone else to take his place. After teaching his brother what he had learned about cooking on Monticello and in France, he was freed in 1796. At the University of Virginia, there is still an original, handwritten list Hemings wrote, cataloging the kitchen equipment before he left. It ranges from sauce pans, to kettles, to dish covers.

President Benjamin Harrison entered the White House with a highly-regarded French chef running the kitchen. Shortly after taking office, he replaced the French chef, Madame Petronard, with Dolly Johnson, a chef who had cooked for his family in their home state of Indiana. It is said that he liked the simplicity of dishes better than the extensive French dishes Madame Petronard had been serving. Similarly, Vietta Garr was the granddaughter of a slave who worked as a chef for the Truman family in Missouri. Upon Truman's election, he asked Garr to come to Washington, D.C. with his family. Instead of simply hiring her as his chef, he wanted her to serve as a mentor for his kitchen staff, in order to teach them how to cook "the Missouri way."

Didn't Want to Know

In an average lifetime, a person breathes in around 45 pounds of dust and debris. More than that, there is more bacteria in a person's mouth than there are people in the United States and Canada combined. A person can grow up to six feet of nose hair in their lifetime. If a man went his entire life without trimming or shaving his beard, it could reach 30 feet long in his lifetime. The ear is more fragile than most people think. In fact, it only takes seven pounds of force to rip off your ear. By the time a person reaches age sixty, they'll have lost around 50% of their taste buds, and, in a lifetime, they can produce enough saliva to fill up two swimming pools.

Survived Times Eight

Queen Victoria once joked that, "It is worth being shot at to see how much one is loved." She of all people should know, as the center of eight assassination attempts. The first came in 1840, shortly after she married Prince Albert. Riding through Hyde Park, 18-year-old Edward Oxford fired a shot at the queen. At first, she did not even realize the shot had been intended for her; she simply thought it was someone hunting nearby. Queen Victoria and Prince Albert just kept riding along in the carriage.

The second and third attempts came just a day apart. On May 29, 1842, a man tried to fire a shot at the queen as she rode to Sunday services at St. James's palace. His pistol failed to fire, and he disappeared. The following day, the same man, John Francis, attempted yet again to shoot the queen. He missed, and he was sentenced to death by hanging. Just five weeks after Francis' attempts, a 17-year-old tried to shoot Queen Victoria on her way from Buckingham Palace to church services. The gun did not fire, and he escaped. The man was found due to a spinal deformity that left him with a hunchback. It is said that the man, John William Bean, was unhappy with his life and looking for a way out.

On the night of her birthday celebration in 1849, the queen was riding with three of her children through Hyde Park. William Hamilton, a bricklayer, fired a shot from almost the exact same spot Edward Oxford had stood nearly a decade earlier. The gun was loaded only with powder, and the queen was left unharmed. Hamilton spent seven years in prison. Robert Pate was already known for his antics around London when he harmed Queen Victoria a year later. He used a cane to hit her on the forehead. Out of all of the assassination attempts, Pate's was the only one to physically injure the queen. She was left with a black eye and a bruise on the right side of her head.

A 17-year-old climbed over the fence at Buckingham Palace in 1872. When Queen Victoria returned from a carriage ride, the man, Arthur O'Connor, rushed and held a gun just a foot away from her. The queen's servant immediately tackled him to the ground, and it was found that the pistol had been broken all along. O'Connor later said that he never planned to actually kill the queen, and that he simply wanted to get her to sign a document that would release political prisons from British jails.

The final assassination attempt took place in 1882, outside of Windsor Station. Crowds cheered for her as she rode past in her carriage, until she saw a crowd of people rushing and tackling a man. She later found out that what she thought was an engine explosion was actually a gunshot. The man who shot her was deemed to be mentally unstable and spent the remainder of his life in an asylum.

The Charts Don't Lie

Margaret Thatcher was a controversial political figure in the United Kingdom. When she died in 2013, a song that had been the anthem for a campaign against her reached number two on the

United Kingdom music charts. The song? "Ding Dong! The Witch is Dead." Some radio stations played the song due to its newfound popularity, while others left it out of rotation out of respect for Thatcher and her family. It became the first song under a minute long to ever make it into the top 10. Other songs in the top five that week? "Need U" by Duke Dumont and A*M*E, "Just Give Me a Reason" by Pink, "Pompeii" by Bastille, and "Feel This Moment" by Pitbull featuring Christina Aguilera.

Inflation Nation

In 2008, Zimbabwe saw an inflation rate unlike anything else in global history. The rate surged to a whopping 231,000,000% in July, which was twenty times higher than just a month before. As a result, shops in the country temporarily accepted South African rands and United States dollars, as the Zimbabwean dollar was worth so little. The government's central bank was forced to remove ten zeros from the currency after having to print $100 billion bills and $100 trillion bills. A year later, twelve more zeroes were taken off the currency. The currency in the country was seen as worthless. After several years of decreasing value, the Zimbabwean dollar was taken out of circulation. To this day, there is no longer an official currency of Zimbabwe, but the central bank allows the use of eight currencies: the South African rand, United States dollar, Chinese yuan, Australian dollar, Indian rupees, Japanese yen,

Botswana pula, and British pounds. The government uses United States dollars for official business, but Zimbabwe residents can open bank accounts in any of the foreign currencies allowed by the central bank.

The Earwax Gene

In humans, there are two earwax types—wet and dry. While nearly 97% of people in Africa and Europe have wet earwax, that number drops to half in places like central Asia and southern Asia. Researches in Japan have found that this is likely due to genetics. There is one gene in DNA that is said to determine whether a person has wet earwax or dry earwax. Researchers believe that the wet form of earwax has been around longer, as it is routed in Africa. Dry earwax was found collectively amongst those in southern Asia. The gene that affects earwax is known as the ATP-binding cassette C11 gene, and there are some theories that suggest a correlation between earwax type and body odor. People who have two A (adenine) versions of the gene have dry earwax, while people who carry two G (guanine) versions of the gene, or one of each, have wet earwax.

Maple Syrup Urine Disease

Maple Syrup Urine Disease may sound like something made up in a cartoon, but it is, in fact, a real disorder. As part of Maple Syrup Urine Disease, the body is unable to break down parts of proteins, which results in the urine smelling like maple syrup. The disorder is inherited and caused by a defect in the genes. While some people suffer from Maple Syrup Urine Disease on a regular basis, others have flare-ups or just mild symptoms. Leucine, isoleucine, and valine are the three amino acids unable to be broken down by people with this condition, and the result is urine that many think have an odor that resembles maple syrup.

Holed In

In Anderson County, Texas, John Joe Gray has withstood what is called the longest-running standoff with police officers in America's history. Gray and his six children have remained holed up in a 47-acre piece of land they own, in a one-sided siege that has taken place for over a decade. It all began when he was arrested for assaulting a state trooper in late 1999 during a traffic stop. A jury indicted him for assaulting a public servant and for taking an officer's weapon. Gray maintained that the patrolmen were lying about the incident and retreated to his property with his family upon being released on bail.

He has remained there ever since and told the officials that they'd need to bring body bags if they ever came to the property to take him into custody. Gray walks around the property with a revolver, rifle, and knife, and his children follow suit. His children range from teenaged Jessica, who keeps a pistol by her side, to 39-year-old Johnathan, who is also armed at all times. Initially, law enforcement officers kept watch over the compound, waiting for a chance to arrest Gray, but they eventually withdrew. The current sheriff of the county has said that he has no intention of going onto the property, just like the three other officials who have held the position of Henderson County Sheriff since the standoff began years ago.

What's the Denomination?

The United States coinage system is one that many say needs an overhaul, when looking at the progress of the rest of the world. People who grow up in the United States are taught that a penny is worth one cent, a nickel is worth five cents, a dime is worth ten cents, and a quarter is worth twenty-five cents. However, unlike most other countries, there is no indication of the denomination written on each coin in numeral form. Sure, the penny says, "One Cent", and the nickel says, "Five Cents," but it has been realized in recent years that this can prove confusing for those with limited literacy or those who are tourists from other countries and cannot read English.

Even the U.S. Embassy to Japan has picked up on the issue. Their website states that they do not know why the United States has coin value words instead of numbers written on their coins, but that it has been this way since the beginning of the coinage system over two-hundred years ago. Furthermore, there is no correlation between size and value. The dime is both smaller and lighter than the nickel, but it is worth twice the amount. A penny is slightly bigger than a dime, despite having one-tenth of the value. It remains a mystery to everyone from elected officials to local consumers. To date, the only United States coin that has the value written out in numbers is the current one-dollar coin, which has "$1" written on the front face.

Animals and Antibiotics

Research has shown that approximately 28.8 million pounds of antibiotics are sold every year in the United States for use in the agriculture sector, while 7 million pounds are sold for human use. That means that 80% of the world's antibiotics are being purchased and used for animals. As antibiotic resistance rises on farms, use of antibiotics intended for humans has become more prevalent amongst animals. Most of these drugs are nearly identical amongst human antibiotics and animal antibiotics.

You Can Rent Anything

In a day and age where people can rent everything from other people's houses, to friends, to brand name clothing, nothing should come as a surprise anymore. Nina Keneally decided to cash in on this rental trend. She started a business after coming to an important realization: many 20-somethings and

30-somethings in the Big Apple need a mother figure in their life. Her company is called Need A Mom, and she charges $40 per hour to any motherly activities, from offering advice, to ironing clothes. She even goes to doctor's appointments with clients who ask, and makes chicken soup for sick clients who request it. The company's motto? "When you need a mom… just not YOUR mom."

Keneally emphasizes that this is not a maid service, and she doesn't simply clean and do laundry. Having raised two children of her own, which she lists amongst her accomplishments on the website, she says she was inspired to start Need A Mom after meeting young people throughout her daily routine—from walking the dog, to partaking in yoga classes—who sought help and guidance. She is located in New York City, which she notes is a key aspect of the business's success. Many younger people move to New York City without their family, so she steps in as that mother figure. In addition to the $40 per hour sessions she offers, Keneally also offers text sessions and letter exchanges. If having a venting session isn't exciting enough, she has also had the distinction of accompanying a client to a colonoscopy procedure.

Once A Snowflake

Before "snowflake" was a term used to describe those who are overly sensitive or coddled, it was simply a term used to describe, well, the snow that fell from the sky. Then, it became a dig used mainly by and toward millennials. Snowflake developed into a mainstream insult in 2016, but its first use can be traced back to 2008. A user on Urban Dictionary defined a snowflake as, "a person who thinks they are OMGUNIQUE!, but, is, in fact, just like everyone else." In May of 2016, the Urban Dictionary definition was changed to, "An overly sensitive person, incapable of dealing with any opinions that differ from their own."

Swooping Season

Magpies are black and white birds that are considered a threat to citizens of their native country, Australia. They often become violent and can peck people at any time. In September and October of each year, a sense of camaraderie sweeps over the country, as residents watch out for one another and warn them about incoming magpies. During this "swooping season," people update maps online that show locations of magpie nests, as well as where attacks have occurred. Radio stations all over the country are sent hundreds of the funniest, most peculiar, and most dramatic magpie swooping stories.

The magpies are considered the biggest problem amongst wildlife in Australia, and citizens have begun to develop some unique means of surviving their swooping season. Students wear ice cream buckets as hats, with drawn-on eyes, in the hopes the magpies won't swoop if they think someone is watching them. Others carry umbrellas all the time, even when it is not raining. An ecologist who has spent over 20 years studying the relationship between humans and magpies has his own favorite method of avoiding the birds: having zip-ties poking out all around your helmet when biking, to keep the magpies away.

Not Quite So High

Mount Everest is known for its abundance of peaks and climbers, but before the days of mountain notoriety, the summit was the seafloor—470 million years ago. The gray limestone on the upper part of Mount Everest was initially part of the continental shelf in Asia during the Paleozoic Era. The rocks from the summit are known as Qomolangma Limestone, and they contain fragments of ancient shells of marine life from the Ordovician Period of the Paleozoic Era.

Toothpick Capital of the World

The town of Strong, Maine, has quite the nickname—Toothpick Capital of the World—bestowed upon them decades ago. Charles Forster, an entrepreneur from Boston, took a trip to Brazil in the mid-19th century when he was first introduced to the concept of a toothpick. Toothpicks had been around for centuries, with the first systemized manufacturing of them taking place in Portugal, but toothpicks made of orangewood soon made their way to Brazil, a colony of Portugal at the time. Forster saw an opportunity. He wanted to create a wooden toothpick that would be accessible to both the rich and the poor.

Forster used shoe pegging equipment as a means of testing out various woods for his project. Along with a shoe pegging mechanic, he finally settled on white birch, as it was both pliable and had a subtle sweet smell and taste. Forster chose Strong, Maine, as his base of operation due to the abundance of trees in the area. The patent for the toothpick was filed in 1885, and the first toothpick mill in the town was opened in 1887. One of Forster's most-used methods to spread word about his toothpicks? He would pay people to request toothpicks in stores and at restaurants. After complaining that the business did not have these exciting new products, Forster would soon visit the location and sell them toothpicks. They became a sign of status, with all of the wealthy men and women chewing on toothpicks at places like restaurants and hotels.

Once business started booming, and Forster was producing over 500 million toothpicks each year, competitors began to emerge throughout the state. Still, Forster's company saw no shortage of success. In the years following World War II, over 75 billion toothpicks were being produced in Strong, Maine, a town with 1,000 residents at the time, each year.

Even the firetrucks in the town were painted with the words "Toothpick Capital of the World" on the side. Nearly 120 years after opening, Forster's toothpick mill closed in 2003, the last in the state to close. Today, no toothpicks are made in Strong, Maine, with the production having moved to other locations all over the world.

No Tattoo for You

While New York City is known for always being ahead of the trend, there is one aspect of popular culture they were slow to catch onto, or, rather, catch *back* onto—tattoos. Tattoos have been a part of the land now known as New York City since the days of the Iroquois tribe. The Native Americans believed tattoos would protect them from evil and provide healing powers. Sailors who passed through New York in the 1700s were also known for getting their initials tattooed on them. In the early 1900s, it is said that more women than men had tattoos in New York City.

However, tattooing became illegal in New York City in 1961, and it wasn't until 1997 that the ban was lifted. No one knows exactly why the ban took place. Some theories include preventing and maintaining an outbreak of hepatitis-B, a secret relationship between a popular tattoo artist's wife and a city official, and the city wanting to maintain a cleaner appearance when they hosted the World's Fair in 1964. Nowadays, there are over 250 tattoo studios in

New York City, and the New York Historical Society Museum and Library had an entire exhibit entitled "Tattooed New York" in early 2017, to share the city's tattoo history.

Different Initials

A study done at University of California at San Diego in 1998 found that there is a correlation between a person's initials and how long they live. The researchers looked at 27 years of death certificates in the state of California and found that people with "unfortunate" initials lived shorter lives. Those 27 years of deaths included approximately 5 million people who died in the state between 1969 and 1997, and focused primarily on men, as men usually don't change their initials upon getting married.

Initials considered to be unfortunate were those like "RAT", "PIG", "ILL", and "BUM", and more desirable initials included "JOY", "WOW", and "GOD". The results showed that men with positive initials lived, on average, 4.48 years longer than the control group, while men with initials of a negative connotation lived 2.8 years less than those in the control group. When looking at the suicide rates, six suicides were noted amongst 1,200 men which "positive" initials, which works out to 0.5%, while the rate increased to 3.5% amongst "negative" initials.

It is uncertain whether or not the results are simply a

coincidence, or if there is, in fact, a direct correlation between initials and lifespan. Some researchers on the project rooted their belief in the relationship between the two on the psychological impact having initials like "RAT" and "BUM" can have, such as low self-esteem and bullying. They say that the results speak for themselves.

Election Thursdays

While there is no definitive reason why elections in England always take place on Thursdays, when asked, different political heads and notable figures throughout England give different reasons as to why this occurs. A British entrepreneur explains that elections took place on any day of the work week— or sometimes even Saturdays—up until 1935. Elections have taken place on Wednesdays every year except two, one of which was when the World Cup started on a Thursday. He reasons that elections take place on Thursdays in today's government because payday is on Friday, and it acts as a reward for completing your duty as a citizen to vote. He believes that if payday were to be on a different day of the week, the election day would reflect that.

Another wealthy entrepreneur, who has even been knighted due to his charitable service, reasons that Thursday is the chosen day for elections simply because it is the most common day for businesses in England to close early, and this gives people more time to get to the polls. E.M. Syddique, a member of the Electoral Reform Society in London, believes the choice of Thursday dates back to 1918, when the Representation of the People Act required that polling be restricted to one day, instead of how it had been, over the course of several days. He believes that Thursday was the furthest day from any possible influences, such as drinking on payday, or being pressured by the clergy at Sunday services.

Other common theories amongst citizens of England? Some think that elections are on Thursdays so that the new Prime Minister has time to choose their Cabinet members—or just celebrate and get drunk—over the weekend, in time to start a new business week on Monday. Others feel that Thursday is simply the day that most people are in town and available to vote. Many people agree with E.M. Syddique, in that Thursday is far enough from Sunday that the church will not have a strong impact on the electors and their voting decisions. Voters and researchers do realize that many of the possible reasons for the Thursday decision are outdated. Thursday was a day for early closing in retail, but now most stores are open seven days a week. Friday was the day for pay packets, which are no longer the common method by which employees are paid. All of these reasons are considered as possibilities for the tradition of Thursday elections, but the government has not given one sole, official reason.

Posthumous Marriage

In April 2017, Xavier Jugelé, a police officer in Paris, was killed in the line of duty. Jugelé had been working on the Champs Elysees for nearly three years when an attacker took his life. He was an active proponent for gay rights and was in a civil partnership with a man named Etienne Cardiles. To honor Jugelé, the first gay posthumous wedding in the country of France—and, presumably, the world—was performed for the couple. Anne Hidalgo, the mayor of Paris, and Francois Hollande, the former President of France, were in attendance. At the time, France was one of the few countries that legally allowed posthumous marriages.

Maple Theft

The year 2012 saw the arrest of three people for a multi-million-dollar theft operation. The thieves were after something highly coveted in Canada: maple syrup. That's right, these men stole nearly $15 million in maple syrup from a Federation of Quebec Maple Syrup Producers storage facility in Quebec, Canada. The warehouse is a co-op between many producers of maple syrup and included around 7,500 syrup producers in the province. The theft was first reported after noticing empty syrup barrels during a routine inventory check, and some barrels that had been drained of syrup and filled with water. The thieves not only stole the syrup, but they also took various pieces of syrup-making equipment.

3.4 million liters of maple syrup was stored in the warehouse, which was over 10% of Quebec's entire harvest for the 2012 season. It was never revealed how much was stolen during the theft, but much of it was sold throughout other parts of Canada and the United States. Over 300 people were interviewed throughout the investigation, with the three arrested on charges of theft, handling stolen goods, fraud, and conspiracy. Nearly five years after the start of the investigation, all three men were sentenced to jail, ranging from two to eight years. The judge ordered that they must also pay fines consisting of millions of dollars over the course of fifteen years.

Newsboys Strike

Before the days of the musical *Newsies,* "newsies" was the nickname given to describe newspaper boys in the late 1800s and early 1900s. In the 1890s, hundreds of young girls and boys sold newspapers throughout New York City. They would be able to purchase a stack of newspapers for 65 cents then spend their days walking up and down the streets, shouting headlines, and advertising their newspapers in an effort to sell them. Selling the papers at one cent each, if the newsies sold their whole stack of newspapers, they made 35 cents.

The price of newspapers jumped from 65 cents to 85 cents in 1898, as a result of the Spanish-American

War. The publisher felt it was easier to sell more papers, as the headlines were more interesting and intriguing to the public. After the war was over, all but two newspaper publishers brought their prices down. Joseph Pulitzer ran *New York Evening World*, while William Randolph Hearst oversaw *New York Evening Journal*. With the increased prices, the newsies had trouble selling their newspapers, and they made a lower profit, making it increasingly difficult for them to survive.

In July of 1899, a small group of the newsies got together and decided that they wanted to boycott the newspapers. They soon convinced hundreds of other newsies to join in their cause. Not only did they stop buying and selling *New York Evening World* and *New York Evening Journal,* they also organized a strike to convince others to stop buying the newspapers. The newsies marched across the Brooklyn Bridge and stopped traffic for several hours, which prevented newspapers from being delivered. Hearst and Pulitzer took notice and struck an agreement with the newspaper boys. While they would not lower their prices back to 65 cents, they would purchase back any newspapers the newsies were unable to sell.

Stole the Volvos

Kim Il-sung was the leader of North Korea in the early 1970s, when Volvo sent marketing materials promoting their then-new 144 GL. Volvo was pushing to be amongst the first European companies to make their way into the North Korean market. Kim Il-sung's regime ordered 1,000 of these new cars, and the first group arrived in North Korea in 1974. Sweden had been working so hard to create ties with North Korea amongst North Korea's economic growth that Volvo didn't realize until an industrial trade fair that the regime had no intention of paying for the vehicles they had purchased. After all, who wouldn't trust the leader of a nation to pay off his debts?

The Swedish media began to cover Kim Il-sung's debts, from the thousand Volvo cars, to over $5 million to Rolex for custom wristwatches. It was then expected that North Korea would pay off their debts in the form of copper and zinc shipments, but the market prices dropped and they were unable to pay up. With inflation factored in, North Korea still owes Sweden nearly $337 million, never having paid off their debts. To this day, the thousand green Volvos are seen on the streets of North Korea, still never having been paid for.

Sperm Sense of Smell

A study done in 2003 aimed to find out more about sperm—specifically, the notion that sperm have a sense of smell. Scientists from the United States and Germany found that an odorant receptor that has been found on sperm is able to direct movement. Thought it is unknown if the compound that attracts the sperm is from the egg or another part of the female reproductive system, researchers do believe that sperm have their own sense of smell, which could prove helpful in fertility treatments. Scientists are still learning more about this receptor, hOR17-4, but they, along with the general public, were surprised to learn that sperm do, in fact, have a sense of smell.

Key to the Ship

The sinking of the Titanic is one of the most well-known nautical tragedies of all time, but some believe that a key element could have prevented it. David Blair was Second Officer on the crew before being removed at the last minute. His superiors had opted to move him off and bring in Henry Wilde, an officer with more experience with large ocean liners. Blair, in the midst of the chaos, forgot to give his replacement a crucial item: a key. Found years later, the key is thought to have been for the locker that contained binoculars for the crew. As the Titanic sailed in the days before sonar technology, the officers on ships like the Titanic had to rely on crow's nest binoculars to detect anything out of the ordinary.

Without the binoculars, members of the ship's crew were unable to see the iceberg until it was too late. One of the lookouts who survived the sinking of the Titanic later said that binoculars would have possibly prevented the tragedy, or at least allowed the lookouts more time to take action. No one knew about the missing key until it was auctioned off 95 years after the ship's sinking. Blair had kept it as a memento and later passed it on to his daughter, who gave it to the British and International Seaman's Society. Some believe that the key was not, in fact, for the binocular locker, but rather for a telephone. As David Blair died in 1955, it is likely that no one will ever know the truth behind the key and what it could have—or could have not—prevented.

The Body is an Amazing Place

If you're looking for one of the wonders of the world, look no further than your own body. The nerve impulses in your body travel at over 429 miles per hour, while a single sneeze generates a gust of wind traveling at 100 miles per hour. A heart beats nearly 30 million times each year, and blood travels around 60,000 miles through your body each day. The pressure your heart creates when it pumps blood is enough to squirt the blood up to 30 feet. Within your body, the average red blood cell can live for 120 days, and there are around 2.5 trillion red blood cells inside your body at any given time.

Between all of the tissue and cells that make up your body, new cells—25 million of them—are being produced every single second. When you smile, you're exercising at least 36 muscles, and the average person produces between four and seven cups of saliva each day. As if that weren't enough, just one square inch of your hand contains 600 pain sensors, 9000 nerve endings, 75 pressure sensors, and nearly nine feet of blood vessels. When you blush, your cheeks aren't the only body part changing colors. Your stomach lining turns red along with your cheeks. By the time you reach age 70, you will have shed, on average, 105 pounds of skin cells.

Strange Mail

Over the years, postal service workers have seen some pretty odd things sent through the mail, ranging from live shrimp to a coffin. One such instance that stands out in the state of Idaho is a "package" sent in 1914 between two towns. May Pierstorff was five years old when her parents spent 50 cents to mail her to her grandparents in Lewiston, Idaho. She was just under 50 pounds, the postal service weight limit at the time. May sat in the mail train car with a clerk from the post office. In the early days of the postal service, "mailing" children was not unheard of, as some parents saw it as a convenient way to transport their children to family members.

Before May, there was a baby boy who was mailed just several weeks after parcel post began in the United States. The baby weighed just over ten pounds and was "mailed" from his parents in Glen Este, Ohio, to his grandparents in Batavia, Ohio. After the parents insured their son and paid 15 cents for the postage stamps, the mail carrier brought the baby to his grandparents. A similar occurrence happened less than a week later in Pennsylvania. A young girl was "mailed" from her parents in Sharpsville, Pennsylvania, to relatives in Clay Hollow, for a total of 45 cents.

Once May Pierstorff's story started spreading, the Postmaster General released a statement banning the mailing of human beings. There are several other stories throughout 1915 of children traveling through the mail system before mail carriers finally took note of the rules. The longest trip of a child through the mail system was made in 1915 by Edna Neff, who was six years old at the time. Her mother sent her off from her home in Pensacola, Florida, and she traveled by a railway mail train to her father in Christiansburg, Virginia. The trip cost just 15 cents. When three-year-old Maud Smith traveled through the postal service to her mother's home in Jackson, Kentucky later that year, an investigation was launched, and the rules were more strictly reinforced.

All for a Bet

Thomas Fitzpatrick was in a tavern in Washington Heights, New York, in September of 1956 when a bet was proposed. Not one to turn down a bet, especially while drinking, Fitzpatrick obliged. The challenge? Get back to the bar from New Jersey in under fifteen minutes. He stole a plane from an airport in New Jersey and flew it into Manhattan, landing on the same street as the bar he had been at, St. Nicholas Avenue. Fitzpatrick took the plane from the Teterboro School of Aeronautics, and flew without radio communication or lighting. The story goes that he had planned on landing on the field at a local high school, but the lights were off, so he opted to land right on the street instead.

As if this feat wasn't impressive—or terrifying—enough, Thomas Fitzpatrick did the exact same thing two years later. After a fellow bar patron said that he didn't believe Fitzpatrick had ever pulled off the stunt, he set off to prove him wrong. This time, he took a plane from Teterboro and landed on 187th and Amsterdam, in front of a school building. After the first incident, he was charged with grand larceny, but the charges were dropped when the owner of the plane opted not to sign a complaint. Once he stole a plane a second time, Fitzpatrick was sentenced to six months in jail on the charge of bringing a stolen item into New York City.

Fitzpatrick was also charged with violating a city code that prohibits the landing of planes on a city street. For this violation, he was only given a fine of $100. Despite the risk he took, people who witnessed the stunt said that Fitzpatrick was a phenomenal flier. After all, he had to be, to land an airplane in the streets of New York City, with cars, lampposts, and people nearby, without harming anyone.

The Great Survival

Gena Turgel's story is one of remarkable fate. She was just sixteen years old when the Nazis invaded her hometown of Krakow, Poland. In the Holocaust, Gena lost her father and seven siblings, including her sister, Miriam, who was shot by the Nazis for smuggling food into Plaszow concentration camp. After spending two years as a prisoner in Plaszow, Gena was sent to Auschwitz. In Auschwitz, she was forced into a gas chamber with hundreds of other prisoners. She was the only one to walk out alive. She hadn't even realized what had happened to her—or that she had been in a gas chamber— until a woman she knew at Auschwitz explained it. She had no voice left and little energy. She survived testing by a Nazi doctor, a death march to Buchenwald, and imprisonment in Bergen-Belsen, before the concentration camps were finally liberated. While each story of survival is remarkable, living to share how you walked in and out of the gas chambers is something very few people in the Holocaust had the fortune of doing.

Whiskey History

Jack Daniel's goes back to the 1870s, when the five-foot-two Jack Daniel decided to make a whiskey with charcoal filtering that could be sold at a premium price. Distilling whiskey was common in Lynchburg, Tennessee, where Daniel resided, as was filtering through charcoal, so he searched for another way to differentiate his whiskey from all the others on the market. Daniel decided on using iron-free spring water from his property, filtered through sugar maple charcoal. This allowed him to produce a smoother, more consistent whiskey.

While Jack Daniel's sales growth was mostly through word of mouth, a feature in *Fortune* in 1951 helped take the whiskey from a local drink to a drink of the stars. It highlighted the many notable people who favored Jack Daniel's, from Winston Churchill to famous Hollywood directors to a Nobel Prize winner. Celebrities like Frank Sinatra and Ava Gardner counted the drink as one of their favorites, with Sinatra even wearing a patch with the logo for a fictional Jack Daniel's Country Club.

Jack Daniel's hit a rough patch in the 1950s through 1970s, where the demand was more than the supply. They promoted their product through advertisements, despite not having the inventory to fulfill orders, and they relied heavily on the image of the common man in Lynchburg to get their brand message across. Jack Daniel's became the drink for the common man. Advertisements featured people in work clothes, and Lynchburg was featured in the photographs. The Jack Daniel Distillery in Lynchburg was opened to the public for tours, with over 200,000 people visiting each year.

Sales tripled for Jack Daniel's between 1973 and 1986, and the growth has continued ever since. The only change in the decades-old process of making the whiskey has been a lowering of the alcohol from 90 proof to 80 proof in 1987. Jack Daniel's now hosts annual barbecue competitions, sponsors racing teams, and even launched a campaign to make Jack's birthday a national holiday in the United States. The whiskey company was also featured in the song "Tik Tok" by Ke$ha, which was the top-selling song of 2010.

Riding and Driving

In the early days of trains, women were discouraged from using them as a means of transportation. The technology was unfamiliar to the public, and it was thought that women's bodies were not made to travel at 50 miles per hour and that their uteruses would physically fly out of their body if they traveled at that speed. There were also theories that people would melt when going at such high speeds. Of course, time and increased travel put these theories to rest, but it didn't end there. When automobiles became more popular in the 1900s, people thought that women would not—and should not—be able to drive them, due to their supposed psychical inferiority and sudden bouts of hysteria. One woman in particular put men's worries at ease. Alice Ramsey was just 22 years old when she drove across the country in 1909. She, along with three friends, drove for 59 days total, and proved that women were just as capable as men were at driving automobiles.

Celebrity Letter Correspondence

Natalie Portman is one of the most popular actresses in Hollywood today, starring in films like *V for Vendetta* and *Black Swan*. When she's not acting, she has another secret talent: she's a master letter writer. Portman has a pen-pal friendship with Jonathan Safran Foer, a best-selling author, known for his books *Extremely Loud & Incredibly Close* and *Everything is Illuminated*. In the days of modern technology—text messages, correspondence via social media—Portman and Foer have maintained their email correspondence for over a decade.

Their friendship began when Foer wrote a book entitled *Eating Animals*, which inspired Portman to become a vegan. She saw him at a book reading, and along with having interest in producing a related movie, wanted to speak with him further. This brought about a friendship centered on letters sent through email. It wasn't until 2016 that the two decided to share some of their emails with the world. One of their more memorable correspondences is when Foer explained his garbage day routine to Portman, explaining that where he lives, Tuesday is the designated day for both garbage and recycling, making it a parking nightmare on his street.

Over the years, the pair has sent, combined, over 2000 messages to one another. They stress that their relationship is not one that is romantic, as Portman is currently married and Foer was married when their correspondence began. Though their early emails to one another were more polished and deep, Portman says that she now emails Foer about whatever is on her mind. She shares that while at the beginning she worked hard to sound smart and impressive, she now feels comfortable sending him everything from thoughts on politics to funny videos online.

Coffee Cups

Every two minutes, people in the United Kingdom go through 10,000 coffee cups. However, what most do not realize is that these paper coffee cups are not recyclable. While most consumers assume that the paper cups are the more eco-friendly choice, most end up in landfills. Because the cups are not made from recyclable material, and they come in contact with the hot coffee or tea, they cannot be put with standard recycling. Technically, because the cups are lined with polyethylene, they can be recycled in a specialty recycling facility, but only two of these exist in the whole United Kingdom. More than that, these facilities have very rarely handled such cups. Each year, in the UK alone, 2.5 billion used coffee cups are thrown in the trash.

Festival of the Steel Phallus

Japan has an annual festival that draws in crowds from all over: the Festival of the Steel Phallus. The annual event has been around since 1969, and, in addition to being a popular event for tourists, helps raise awareness about safe sex, celebrates fertility, and raises funds for HIV research. Steel phallus statues line the streets and parades abound the city of Kawasaki. Everything from phallus-shaped vegetables to phallus keychains are out in full swing.

It all dates back to the 17th century, with a legend that has been told for generations. The legend goes that a demon was hiding inside the vagina of a woman who didn't reciprocate his feelings of love, and the demon bit off the phallus of her husband as revenge. The same thing happened with her second husband. The woman wanted to break the spell, so she worked with a blacksmith to create a steel phallus, in an effort to break the curse—and the teeth of the demon.

North Sentinel Island

North Sentinel Island is a small island in the Indian Ocean the size of Manhattan. Owned by the government of India, visitors are not allowed within three miles of the island for their own protection. The indigenous people of North Sentinel Island do not take kindly to outsiders, as they're used to the seclusion of their own island. In 2006, two fishermen lost their way and found themselves on the island. They were immediately killed by residents of the island. Not much is known about the island, other than this incident, due to the lack of tolerance of outsiders, as well as the many forests that cover most of the island. No one even knows how many people live on the island, though it is estimated to be less than a few hundred. Based on research done by anthropologists, the tribe has been indigenous to North Sentinel Island for approximately 60,000 years. Outside governments have tried to make contact with the residents, but, as they have been hostile in return, have decided to leave them be. They are thought to be one of the only remaining tribes or groups of people without any aspect of modern civilization.

An Oatful Experiment

In the late 1940s and early 1950s, the Fernald School in Massachusetts was a school for mentally disabled and abandoned children. Students were not treated well, so members of the Science Club were excited when they started being fed cereal for breakfast each morning. What they didn't know was that they were part of an experiment, and that the Quaker oatmeal they were being served contained radioactive tracers. It took almost forty years before the boys in the club found out the truth.

Robert Harris, a nutrition professor at MIT, oversaw three experiments with over 70 boys from the school, all between ages 10 and 17. One of these experiments involved feeding the boys oatmeal and milk that were laced with radioactive nutrients, while another saw him directly injecting radioactive calcium into the boys. A third experiment dealt with calcium and the bloodstream. These experiments had both been approved by the Atomic Energy Commission, as were dozens of other experiments in the same time period. Quaker had decided to team up with scientists in order to have another way to market their products. They were in heavy competition with Cream of Wheat, whose product, unlike theirs, did not impact the absorption of iron.

With nutrition becoming a huge selling point in the early 1950s, Quaker provided funding for the experiment, along with the free breakfast cereal. The boys at the Fernald School ate the oats with radioactive tracers, which are used to help assess chemical reactions within the body, and it was found that the Quaker oats were not any worse when it came to absorbing calcium and iron than Cream of Wheat was. The boys who were used as test subjects in these experiments did not find out about the experiments until 1993, when the Secretary of Energy removed the classified status of several documents from the Atomic Energy Commission.

Upon learning of this testing, thirty students who had unknowingly taken part sued Quaker Oats and MIT. The focus point of the case was that Robert Harris and Quaker Oats had preyed on vulnerable boys with no families to look out for them, and it was questioned why they had not used test subjects from other schools or from MIT. A physics professor at MIT argued in front of the Senate that the experiment exposed the boys to trace amounts of radiation and not enough to have done any long-term damage to them. President Clinton issued an apology to the students in 1995, as the Atomic Energy Commission, a federally-funded agency that has since become defunct, had funded the study. A settlement of $1.85 million was eventually reached, but Quaker admitted no wrongdoing.

Meat Allergy

Red meat allergies, also known as alpha-gal syndrome, have been on the rise in recent years. Alpha-gal, which stands for Galactose-alpha-1, 3-galactose, is a molecule found in meats like beef, pork, and lamb. Research has found a connection between this red meat allergy and tick bites, most commonly what's known as the lone star tick. The theory is that these ticks feast on raw meat from deer carcasses and transfer the alpha-gal to the humans, developing a molecule that is connected to the red meat allergy. In the first several months of 2017 alone, there was a 7.5% increase of patients being treated by allergists for alpha-gal syndrome, and red meat allergies are more common than ever.

LAPD Helicopters

Police helicopters play a pivotal role in the success of the police force in Los Angeles, and the LAPD helicopter fleet is now the biggest fleet of police helicopters in the United States, with 17 choppers. Over the course of the year, the helicopters do a combined 18,000 hours of flight, observing crime, serving as backup for officers on the ground, and ensuring stability of infrastructure. The Hooper Heliport, west of the Los Angeles River, is where most of the choppers take off and land. LAPD helicopters have helped set up perimeters for ground officers to surround and maintain a crime scene, and they also served as backup for ground officers around 4,000 times each year. While it is hard to measure the exact impact the fleet of choppers has on the city of Los Angeles, they helped recover 6% of recovered vehicles that had been stolen in 2011, and, in the same year, they provided support with one in every seven felony arrests. It costs $20 million to run and maintain the fleet of helicopters each year.

A Family Affair

Uein Buranibwe and Temaei Tontaake were lost at sea for 33 days in 2012 before washing up on one of the Marshall Islands. Over 350 miles from home, their GPS had stopped working, and they were surviving on fish they were catching. On Namdrik Island, the two were given food and water, but, more than that, they reconnected with family. One of the men found out that his uncle, who his family presumed had drowned fifty years earlier, had actually washed up on the same island. He had married a local and lived out his life on the island. Although the uncle had since passed, the man got to meet relatives he never knew existed. What a reward for surviving nearly five weeks lost at sea!

Obsession with Perfection

A study revealed that the amount of food Americans eat is nearly equivalent to the amount of food they throw away. Americans tend to have an idea that fresh produce should be blemish-free, and many consumers, supermarkets, and packers refuse produce items that appear imperfect. Approximately one-third—and $160 billion—of produce is wasted each year. The cycle starts early on. Instead of letting blemished fruits and vegetables go through the packing, shipping, trucking, and distributing processes, many farmers will simply leave the vegetables and fruits in the field, instead of incurring expenses and labor needs that will later have been wasted.

Some farmers estimate that they throw away or feed cattle around one-quarter of their crops, but the amount can vary based on crop, season, and appearance. If oranges have a rip in the peel, people will not buy them. If cauliflower is darker because of the sun, consumers presume something is wrong with it. The amount of food wasted each year is enough to feed everyone in all five boroughs of New York, plus Jersey City and Newark. Many grocery stores will not even purchase such produce, because consumers have the notion that produce must look perfect. Companies like Imperfect Produce and Food Cowboy have been started with the goal of finding a use for scarred and blemished produce, but the root of the problem still remains with American consumers.

Conjoined

While some parents of conjoined twins decide to keep their children together due to the risks involved, others opt to have their children undergo separation surgery. Angelina and Angelica Sabuco were born conjoined with their chests and abdomen attached. At the age of two, the conjoined twins were separated in a surgery that lasted ten hours. Dividing the liver the girls shared was the most complex and concerning part of the surgery, but it went smoothly, and the girls now live in separate bodies. In Chile, Maria Paz and Maria Jose underwent separation surgery at 10 months old. The surgery took eight hours and involved over twenty surgeons and anesthesiologists. The twins were conjoined more complexly, at the stomach, pelvis, and thorax. Both twins survived the surgery, but Maria Paz passed away four days later as a result of organ failure.

Rital and Ritag Gaboura were given one-in-ten-million odds of surviving a separation surgery. Joined at the head, their surgery was complex due to the blood vessels they shared and the blood flow that ran through both of their brains. They were separated in September 2011. As the surgery was done at 11 months of age, it was too early to tell if the surgery made any impact on brain activity for the girls. Fiorella and Yurelia Rocha-Arias were considered high-risk when they underwent separation surgery at the age of three. From Costa Rica, the family came to New York for the surgery, where the largest team of doctors in the hospital's history successfully separated them. The two now live independent lives, running separately, sitting in their own chairs, and living without an attached chest area.

Lakshmi Tatma had a truly unique case. She was one of a set of conjoined twins joined at the pelvis, but her twin never fully formed and was headless, leaving her with the appearance of having four arms and four legs. While some people in her village in India thought this meant she was the reincarnation of a Hindu goddess, she underwent surgery at the age of two. The operation took 27 hours, and Lakshi resumed a normal life after the surgery.

Clarence and Carl Aguirre were born in the Philippines in 2002. They were just like any other set of twins—except they were attached at the head. Their mother, Arlene, brought them to America, hopeful that doctors would be able to separate them. For one of the first times ever, doctors opted to separate the Aguirre twins over the course of several smaller surgeries, as opposed to the hours-long surgeries that had been done on conjoined twins up until that point. The first surgery was performed in October 2003, with tissue expanders being implanted in their scalps, with the goal of creating extra skin to be used in the separation. The final surgery took place in August 2004, after their skulls had been slowly moved apart. Carl was left with permanent disabilities and uses a wheelchair to get around. By the age of twelve, he could speak just a few words at a time. Both boys still wear helmets to protect their fragile skulls.

Dunk No More

While all of the greatest sports movies and television shows may highlight slam dunks, many who watch and play the game on a collegiate level are against dunking. For years, from the 1930s to the 1980s, people talked of banning slam dunks or raising the rim to make it impossible—or at least more difficult—to dunk. While basketball players had an average height of 5 feet, 10 inches in 1940, the average height grew when teams realized that they could simply acquire tall players to stand near the hoop and either get the rebounds or dunk the basketball. These players were referred to as "goal tenders," and players were making upwards of a dozen blocks per game. The goaltending rule was finally put into effect in 1944. Four rules were changed in the NCAA, including the banning of goaltending and the banning of passing over the backboard.

Wilt Chamberlain entered the game in 1956 and stirred up talks of changes for rim height. Baskets had become so easy for players of his height that fans were starting to lose interest in the game. Dunking was officially banned in the NCAA in 1967, as a star player from UCLA, Lew Alcindor—now known as Kareem Abdul-Jabbar—dominated every game with his height. With standard basketball rim height sitting at ten feet, coaches also tried to have the rim raised to twelve feet, and some even suggesting it be raised to fourteen feet. The dunking ban was ultimately lifted in 1976, but the controversy has remained. A magazine in the early 1980s compared slam dunking to how gorillas in a zoo would play basketball, and coaches still regularly call for the moving up of the rim.

Ukraine Without "The"

When President Obama delivered a speech and mentioned the country of Ukraine, he learned an important lesson: the proper way to say the country's name is "Ukraine", not "the Ukraine". Many journalists and officials have made the same mistake. As a former US ambassador to Ukraine explains, Russia used to refer to the area as "the Ukraine" when the Soviet Union was in charge. Now that Ukraine is its own country, there is no longer a "the" before the country's name. Ukrainians take the blunder as an insult, and they find it very upsetting.

Fat Chance

We've all heard it before… you're going to get food poisoning if you eat raw eggs or undercooked meat. But most consumers tend to ignore the rule, and new research has shown that they may be right. If a person eats two eggs per meal, twice a week, for their entire lives, they still only have a 1 in 625 chance of eating an egg with salmonella. The USA and FDA mandate recalls for any outbreaks that occur, often causing panic amongst locals wherever the recall is located. However, most consumers have taken an "if it happens, it happens" attitude about food poisonings. The easiest way to avoid food poisoning like E. coli? Common sense. Use a meat thermometer, don't eat undercooked meat, and don't worry too much. Even if you eat two hundred burgers each year, the odds are only 1:50 of you having an E. coli infection in your lifetime.

Made in the USA

Walmart found itself in hot water in 2015 when it was revealed that they had mislabeled their products as "Made in the USA." Many consumers were upset with this realization, as some choose to purchase only American-made products and feel that this was false advertising. The two main items caught up in this controversy were Equate products, part of Walmart's own line of beauty and healthcare products. Equate makeup sponges had a label that read "Made in the USA," despite also having another clear label reading "Made in China." The Equate 7-Day Whitening Wraps were also listed as being made in the United States, despite the Walmart website saying that the product had been imported.

Walmart responded by saying that it had only been recently that manufacturing for the products involved was moved to the United States, and that some stores may have simply still had the older versions in stock. Products beyond just the store's own brand were being mislabeled in the store and on the website. Almay eyeliner says right on the packaging that it is from Germany, but Walmart still gave it the "Made in the USA" tag. A representative for Walmart followed up by saying that they are simply working to improve the accuracy of listings on their website, and that the mistakes only applied to a few select items.

Bad to the Bone

While the term "bone china" is commonly used when picking out serving dishes and place settings for a house, most people don't know the origin behind the term. Bone china is named as such because it does, in fact, have bone ash inside of it. The process of making bone china dates back to the 18th century, when a man in England came up with a new way to create china that involved calcined bone ash. It was thought that this new formula would be stronger than simple porcelain, and, over the years, bone china has still maintained a reputation as one of the finest porcelain products. Companies like Lenox — the only one in the United States — still make bone china, all based on this idea of bone ash that began several hundred years ago.

Mr. Plastic Fantastic

In 2016, Walter Cavanagh inadvertently set a world record. Guinness World Record bestowed the title of "Mr. Plastic Fantastic" on Cavanagh as the person in the world with the most credit cards to his name. Cavanagh, who was 73 years old at the time of his achievement, has a whopping 1,497 credit cards to his name, which totals a $1.7 million combined credit limit. He says that he does not carry all credit cards on him at all times, and he mainly uses one card, which he pays off each month. Cavanagh's credit score has not taken a hit due to the massive number of credit cards, as he says his credit score is nearly perfect. The credit cards in Cavanagh's name vary greatly in spending limits, from just $50 upward. He started collecting credit cards as a bet with a friend. His 1,497 credit cards are a far cry from the national average of two credit cards per person.

Whiskey Benefits

Besides being known for getting you buzzed, whiskey has some surprising health benefits, and it is considered one of the healthier forms of alcohol.

While whiskey must, of course, be consumed in moderation, it is relatively low in carbohydrates, cholesterol, and sodium. Whiskey is thought to help more with weight loss than other alcohols, like beer, due to the lack of fat, and the simple sugars it contains being broken down into energy. Studies have even shown that people who drink small amounts of whiskey on a regular basis have a nearly 50% less chance of having a heart attack or stroke.

Whiskey has also been found to reduce clotting of blood, as it is considered a blood thinner. The drink also contains high levels of ellagic acid, an antioxidant compound that helps prevent diseases and even possibly reduce chances of cancer and premature aging. The antioxidants also help with the immune system, whose job it is to fight against colds and infections. Ellagic acid is known for being able to fight against free radicals inside the body, which can slow the effects of dementia or reduce the likelihood of suffering from dementia and Alzheimer's. Consuming moderate amounts of whiskey can also aid in your body's capability of regulating levels of insulin, which is thought to reduce the odds of getting diabetes by up to 30-40%.

All for The Poop

In the 1860s, animal guano—or bird poop—was a hot commodity. It was the most popular export of Peru, and nearly 60% of the country's economy depended on it. The seabird and bat guano came primarily from the Chincha Islands, a group of islands near Peru, and Luis Hernandez Pinzon, a Spanish admiral, became angry at the success they were having with this export. Pinzon sent in hundreds of marines to take control of the Chincha Islands, which included arresting the governor at the time and appointing his own governor. Nearby South American countries feared that this was just the beginning of Spain's mission to reclaim all of its former colonies, so they banded together to fight against Spain.

The war lasted two years, with Pinzon blocking all ports in Peru, governments being torn apart, and the economies of several countries being completely destroyed. Chile declared war on Spain in September of 1865, after a Spanish ship sailed into a port in Chile in order to replenish their supplies. They banded together with their neighbor, Peru, and had an early victory against Spain—despite Spain's power—when they captured and imprisoned an entire ship crew. Bolivia and Ecuador joined the war soon after. The Spanish destroyed the majority of Peru's fleet, and it took the country years to recover. Finally, the Spanish admiral considered the circumstances and decided the war was no longer worth it. They quietly retreated, and it took twenty years before reconnecting with the countries involved. All of this—a war and destruction— for some bird and bat droppings.

A Different Kind of Thief

Toilet paper theft has become an increasingly large problem in parts of Beijing, China, over the course of the past several decades. Temple of Heaven Park has decided to take matters into their own hands by installing facial recognition software in the bathroom stalls. If a visitor needs toilet paper in the bathroom, they must first look into a computer, which has the software installed. The computer is programmed to recognize faces and only give someone one use's worth of toilet paper. If someone needs more toilet paper, they must wait nine minutes.

The biggest culprits of toilet paper theft, according to those in the area, seem to be older people, who will stuff their purses and bags with unused toilet paper, in order to take it home and avoid having to purchase any. While some feel that this new installation is an invasion of privacy and unnecessary, others think it is a great addition to the park and was long overdue. There are many public bathrooms throughout China that expect visitors to bring their own toilet paper, but areas that attract more tourists have gotten on board with providing toilet paper for visitors.

Angel's Glow

The Battle of Shiloh took place during the Civil War in 1862. As soldiers tended to their wounds, they realized that the wounds were faintly glowing with a blue color. No one knew the reason, but, as those with the glowing wounds seemed to survive more than those without the glow, it was named "Angel's Glow". The cause of this glow remained a mystery for over a century, until a 17-year-old took a trip to the battlefield in 2001. Having heard the stories surrounding Angel's Glow, Bill Martin was curious as to what causes the blue glow. His mother was a microbiologist studying bacteria in soil that let off a faint blue color, and he began to wonder if this could be what caused the Angel's Glow.

Bill, along with his friend Jonathan, researched the P. luminescens bacterium, which can only survive in cooler temperatures. They concluded that soldiers had been on the cold, possibly wet ground for days, which could have easily lowered their body temperature. Their theory became that the bacteria saved the men's lives by eliminating more harmful bacteria and cleaning out the wounds. While no one can say with 100% certainty that this is the cause of Angel's Glow, it is the only theory that scientists and researchers agree makes sense for the situation.

Feathers Wherever

Chicken feathers have become a popular material in all sorts of products. While bird feathers are commonly thought of in things like feather pillows and boas, chicken feathers aren't quite the right material to provide warmth, so they are not amongst the bird feathers used for such products. Six billion tons of feathers are produced—and generally thrown away—by the poultry industry each year, but the amount being discarded has been reduced due to one chemist's idea in 1993.

Walter Schmidt made an arrangement with Perdue Farms and Tyson Foods, two of the biggest poultry producers, to obtain all of their chicken feathers. Along with his colleagues, Schmidt performed tests on the feathers and made all sorts of creations with them. He created the first paper made out of chicken feathers, and other products like dishes, clothing items, and furniture. Schmidt and his colleagues found that chicken feathers have keratin, which produces strong proteins and provides a biodegradable option to some plastics.

The work done by this group of chemists has provided inspiration for others to make their own creations. A group of students at the University of Delaware created shoes made of chicken feathers, soybeans, and natural fibers. One woman in Oregon opened a business selling feathers from her own chickens to jewelry makers, hat designers, and artists. Groups are working on all sorts of new product ideas and patents to utilize chicken feathers, which they believe is the material of the future.

Mobile Subway

When the World Trade Center was being rebuilt in the early 2010s, Subway decided it was the perfect location for a new Subway shop. This shop was a mobile shop that moved up each story as the construction continued along. It was built because workers generally had a thirty-minute lunch break, but it took them longer than that entire break just to wait for the construction elevators to take them to ground level. The temporary Subway location— which lasted for around two years—looked as if it were hanging without a sound structure. Several other businesses were considered for the operation, but many of them were unable to make it work with the unique circumstances, or simply uncomfortable doing so. The Subway store served more than just Subway foods, with typical New York lunch fare making its way onto the menu.

Trapped in an Elevator

Nicholas White's life changed when he was trapped in an elevator in 1999. He was working as a production manager for a magazine when he went out for a smoke break one Friday night while he was working late. White got back into the elevator after his smoke break, only to have the elevator shake and stop moving. As lights began flashing, White's first thoughts were about the inconvenience, not knowing how long it would take.

Nicholas White was stuck in the elevator for a total of 41 hours. The rest of his account came through surveillance footage of the occurrence. White's initial confusion changed to panic, as he tried to press buttons and get the intercom to work. The alarm only provided a higher sense of terror, as it was a loud noise that continued consistently, and he ended up pulling off the alarm button entirely. After hours of pacing back and forth, White was finally able to pry the doors open. He came face-to-face with a cinderblock wall that had the number 13 written on it.

White could be seen on surveillance footage doing anything he could to pass the time. He sorted through everything in his wallet, attempted to use his shoes as pillows, and went to the bathroom in the elevator shaft. Without a cell phone or watch, he had no way of communicating with anyone and no clue how much time had passed. White was finally helped and freed from the elevator on Sunday afternoon. He filed a $25 million lawsuit against both the elevator maintenance company and the management of the building he worked at. Security footage showed other elevators in the building undergoing routine maintenance, and it is unknown why his elevator car was not given the same treatment.

After missing eight weeks of work, White was fired from his job. It took four years for the lawsuit to be settled, and the sum, which was never revealed, was said to be minimal. White suffered from horrible anxiety and hallucinations, and he said this hindered his ability to find and keep work. Reflecting on his decision to file a lawsuit, White said years later that he regretted it, and that he should have gone back to his job. The 41 hours he spent stuck in an elevator stay with him on a daily basis, but, as a resident New Yorker, he is unable to avoid elevators.

Chang and Eng's Civil War

Chang and Eng Bunker are one of the most famous pairs of conjoined twins, but that didn't excuse them from the draft during the Civil War. Born in Thailand, the Bunkers had found work in a sideshow, with people paying simply to see this phenomenon of two people being joined at the sternum. At the start of the Civil War, they had recently retired from the sideshow and were living in the town of Traphill, North Carolina. When George Stoneman, a Union general, raided their town, he created a lottery of all men over the age of 18 in order to choose who would serve with him. Eng Bunker's name was drawn, while Chang's was not. The possibility of separating the twins was even brought up, but it was deemed impossible because their livers were attached. Thus, the Bunkers were excused from serving in the war, and General Stoneman told his troops to leave the twins and their property alone.

Legal Loophole

Genene Jones became one of the most hated women in southern Texas when she was convicted of murdering a 15-month-old while working as a pediatric nurse. Many believe her crimes could have been prevented. Long before she was convicted of killing Chelsea McClellan, Jones had arisen suspicion because a high number of children has begun dying while she was on duty. It got to the point where her shift was called the "Death Shift." Instead of reporting her, the hospital she was working at simply moved her to a different department.

When she worked at a different medical clinic, eight children who had been under the care of Genene Jones had emergencies arise. Chelsea McClellan was then in her care, and she was given two doses of a muscle relaxer that causes cardiac arrest. In addition to eyewitnesses testifying against Jones, researchers were able to create a system to measure traces of the drug she had given Chelsea. Enough of the drugs were found to send Jones to prison. It is believed that she played a role in the deaths of many more children—dozens, at least— but there was never enough evidence to convict.

What's more shocking than the crimes she committed is the fact that a legal loophole might allow Jones, who was sentenced to 99 years in jail, to be released. The loophole? A law in Texas that allows sentences to be reduced by up to two-thirds of the sentence time, in order to prevent overcrowding in the prisons. As Jones was convicted of the murder in 1984, she may be released in 2018.

Cold Case Confession

Trevell Coleman began made a name for himself as G. Dep, but not without hiding some skeletons in his closet. In 1993, when he was 18 years old, Coleman was addicted to drugs and making money as a cocaine dealer. He bought a gun and used it to mug a stranger. When the man put up a fight, Coleman fired three times and fled the scene. The following day, police in the neighborhood were going around asking people if they had heard anything about a shooting the previous night. This made Coleman believe that the man had not died, so he kept his involvement in the shooting a secret, never sharing the details with anyone.

Coleman continued to try his hand at a rap career, and several years after the shooting, he caught the attention of P. Diddy. He signed a record deal and continued to be mentored by P. Diddy, but the night of the shooting always stayed with him. Once he became a father, he began to wonder about the man he had shot and if he'd had children. In 2010, wrought with guilt, Coleman walked into a police station and told a police officer he had shot someone over a decade earlier. The officer did nothing about it.

Still, Coleman went back two weeks later and spoke with another officer. This time, he shared the few details he could remember, including a description of the victim and the location of the shooting. He could not remember the date, but the police found a match in the cold case files. John Henkel had been shot on October 19, 1993, and had died at the scene. It wasn't until the police told him that Coleman knew the man he had shot had died. Coleman was charged with murder and sentenced in 2012 to fifteen years to life. He maintains that he does not regret turning himself in.

Playoff Beards

One of the main—or, at least, favorite—indicators that it's playoff season in hockey is the increase in facial hair amongst players. The tradition originated in the 1980s, when the New York Islanders grew beards during their playoff run, resulting in four Stanley Cups. Bob Nystrom, who was a forward on the team when the tradition originated, said it wasn't something that they planned as some sort of team activity, and that it was just a random occurrence. The Islanders lost semifinal games in the years leading up to their Stanley cup reign, but finally won four years in a row, which happened to coincide with when they grew out their facial hair. In 1984, the same year they abandoned the tradition, the Islanders lost to the Edmonton Oilers. With a myth of correlation between facial hair and wins, many professional hockey players have opted to grow out their beards during playoff season.

Hyder, Alaska

Hyder, Alaska, was known as a mining town decades ago. Now, it is so far off the grid that residents band together to place large orders of food and try to place online orders in groups for convenience and shipping charges. Mail only flies into the town twice a week—so long as the weather is nice—and there is only one road into and out of the town. With just 87 residents, Hyder is considered to be a ghost town, and there are just two saloons, a bar, a few stores, and a post office in the town. Residents send their children to a school in nearby Stewart, British Columbia, which is also the town with the closest grocery store. In Hyder, seeing bears around the town and experiencing blizzards are normal occurrences.

Hyder is the easternmost town in the state of Alaska, but its rules and traditions take on that of another country. They accept Canadian currency, implement no American policies, and have no police forces or property taxes. The small village relies on towns in nearby British Columbia, notably Stewart, for services like electricity. Despite being small in area and population, Hyder has plenty of celebrations, like an annual pet parade, an ugly vehicle contest, and a contest called the Bush Woman Classic, which involves flipping pancakes, catching fish, and putting on lipstick. Throughout the summer months, over 100,000 people visit the area of Hyder and

Stewart, to enjoy the outdoors and visit nearby monuments.

Days of the Dinosaur

Films like *Jurassic Park* have long intrigued Florida residents, who question where they can visit archaeological sites and see dinosaur remains. When Jurassic Park Orlando opened in Florida in the 1990s, scientists received hundreds of phone calls from people asking where the dinosaurs in the film could have been found. Unfortunately for them, the answer was nowhere. Florida is one of the few states that had zero dinosaurs roaming around millions of years ago. The reason is simple: Florida was completely under water during that time. Animals from thousands of years ago, like mammoths and mastodons, are believed to have roamed southern Florida, but dinosaurs were not in the area. Florida was under water until roughly 30 million years ago, while dinosaurs were in existence between 65 and 225 million years ago. While reptiles lived in the sea where Florida now stands, paleontologists say that these were not true dinosaurs. The closest location to Florida where a dinosaur fossil has been found is Columbus, Georgia. Fossils have been found throughout the state of Florida, but these have been for animals that came millions of years after dinosaurs, like sea turtles, tortoises, and large ground sloths.

Disney Intimates

Before Disneyland was such a family-friendly tourist destination, a unique store was located on Main Street. The Intimate Apparel Shop, part of Hollywood-Maxwell Brassiere Company, was opened in 1955, with brassieres, corsets, and petticoats. The store made headlines in publications ranging from the Long Beach Press-Telegram to the Santa Ana Register, advertising its featuring of an 1860 Singer Sewing Machine and the Wizard of Bras, a mechanical wizard that wore both clothes from the 1890s and modern-day clothes from the 1950s.

An article in *The Disneyland News*, a small monthly newspaper that was run by Disneyland, had a headline that read, "If Hubby Is Shy, Watch Him at Main Street Corset Shop." The article went on to explain how bashful most men would get when walking into the store, while young girls surprisingly loved visiting the store for its old-school feel and furnishings. The shop became known for being both a contemporary shopping experience and a tribute to the fashion of the past. The Intimate Apparel Shop closed less than two years after it was opened, and the Victorian building in which it was located has been home to a china and figurine store ever since.

History of Hypnosis

Today, hypnosis is used as a psychological technique, and—let's be honest— sometimes as a party or event activity. Hypnosis dates back thousands of years, with documents supporting the idea that a form of hypnosis was round in the days of the Ancient Greeks, Romans, Persians, and Egyptians. At that time, it was used to cure both physical ailments and emotional disorders. Some researchers believe that hypnosis is even older, as cave paintings can be interpreted as having priests in a trance, with geometric shapes around them, presumably to depict various levels of consciousness.

Modern day hypnosis came to be amongst Islamic scientists in the 9th through 14th centuries. They took the knowledge passed on from ancient civilizations and began to understand more about psychology and the idea of various states of consciousness. Dr. Frantz Anton Mesmer was a physicist in Austria in the 18th century, who was amongst the first to stimulate a trance-like condition through the use of magnets and magnetic forces. Doctors and other medical professionals ostracized Mesmer, believing that his work was merely theatrics, due to there being no tangible results. His work in the field—and his name—gave us the word "mesmerize". In the late 19th century, Sigmund Freud began work with hypnosis, and it is believed that he quickly moved on from the idea of hypnosis because he did not have the patience to learn the trade.

Following World War I, hypnosis became a common method of treating soldiers who had suffered trauma during their time in the military. This brought about new attention to the method of psychology. Hypnosis wasn't approved as an official medical treatment and tool until 1955 in the United Kingdom and 1958 in the United States. Years later, the first full-time hypnosis physician, William J. Bryan, Jr., founded the American Institute of Hypnosis. Hypnosis has become a popular self-help method, and has entered the mainstream through means of video tapes and the internet.

Pressing Your Luck

A study was done in 2012 to break down the demographics of those who purchase lottery tickets in the United States. Men were found to play the lottery much more frequently than women, with 18.7 days per year for men, compared to 11.3 days per year for women. A whopping 79% of those between the ages of 20 and 39 play the lottery in any given year, while the number decreases to 66% for those ages 40-69, and 45% for people aged 70 and over. Native Americans were found to have the highest average when it comes to days of gambling, with the average reaching 25 days each year. They also, along with Caucasians, had the highest percentage of people—over 50%— who had played the lottery in the previous year. Amongst the lowest one-fifth, based on socioeconomic status, 61% of people had gambled throughout the course of the past year, with an average of 26.1 days. For the top three levels of socioeconomic status, the percentage dropped to just 42%, with 10 days of gambling.

Pay for Your Pew

Churches in the 19th and 20th centuries had a tradition that many today would scoff at: they would charge parishioners rent for their pews. Members would pay an annual rent, which would allow them to sit in the same pew each week at Sunday services. Not all pews at a church would be rented, to allow people who opted not to pay the rental fee to come and pray, but it is believed that many of the unrented pews were further in the back and without cushioned seating. At Saint Mark's Church in Philadelphia, a meeting about pew rental was recorded in 1947. It went into detail about the privileges that those who opted to rent pews should have, while also explaining that the reservation of pews did not apply to special occasions and holidays. Pews in the front traditionally cost more to rent, as they had better access to the sound and a better view.

Senate Candy Desk

While food is generally not allowed in the US Senate chamber, George Murphy, a California senator, started a unique tradition in the 1960s. Murphy began to fill one of the drawers in his desk with candy and sneak pieces of candy from the desk throughout the day. Each time a colleague would catch him with his candy, he would share in order to get them to keep quiet. Word spread of this unique situation, and people responded favorably to the idea of having a secret hiding place for sweet treats in one of the senator's desks. Despite Murphy's defeat in the 1970 elections, senators continued on with his innovation and continued to stock the desk drawer with candy. The tradition has lived on through the years, with senators including Paul Fannin from Arizona, Steve Symms from Idaho, and Rick Santorum from Pennsylvania having taken on the role of keeper of the candy.

Steve Symms brought new life to the tradition when he strayed from the hard candy that had always filled the desk, and began to include chocolates from Idaho in the rotation. The practice of keeping a candy drawer was revealed by Slade Gorton, a senator who had been assigned to the candy desk, in 1985. Though the candy desk has switched locations based on the senator chosen for the role, it has remained in the same spot since 1981, due to its proximity to the eastern entryway. Pat Toomey, a senator from Pennsylvania, is the current occupant of the candy desk. Like Santorum, he often fills the drawer with products from Pennsylvania-based candy companies, like Hershey's and Just Born.

The Seven-Five

The 75th Precinct of the NYPD in Brooklyn saw one of the most shocking cases of corruption and cover-up between 1986 and 1992. Michael Dowd, a police officer at the precinct, was the leader of a group of corrupt officers known for robbing drug dealers and selling drugs. The wrongdoing was obvious, with Dowd flaunting his newfound money, being picked up in limousines, driving a Corvette, and taking regular trips to Atlantic City casinos. Many of Dowd's superiors ignored what he was doing, for fear that the charges of corruption under their command could ruin their careers. Investigations within the 75th precinct were intentionally thrown in order to close the cases and avoid finding anything that could reveal the misconduct. It wasn't until Dowd was arrested in Suffolk County for conversations with a drug dealer that the rest of the corruption was revealed.

In 1988, a grocery store that was a known front for drug operations was held up by three officers from the same precinct—the 75th. The officers were charged once the drugs and money that had been stolen were found in their car. Despite rumors that Officer Dowd was involved in the heist, nothing was ever done about it. Drug dealers testified that they were paying Dowd up to $4,000 each week, in addition to some cocaine, in order to keep him from arresting them. No investigation into Dowd was opened by Internal Affairs until the Suffolk County arrest. Dozens of fellow officers and superiors had simply looked the other way.

A Long Anthem

The national anthem of Greece is based off a poem, "Hymn to the Freedom," written by Dionysios Solomos. It was inspired by the events of the Greek Revolution in 1821, when Solomos was just 25 years old. Though the version sung today is just one verse, the entire Greek national anthem is much longer: 158 verses. "Hymn to the Freedom" has been praised for decades due to its patriotic nature, so a shorter, three stanza version is what has been used as the national anthem since 1865.

Alcatraz of the Rockies

While Alcatraz has long been thought of as one of the worst prisons in United States history, home to only the most horrible offenders, another prison has been making a name for itself. The US Penitentiary Administrative Maximum Facility, also known as ADX, is now the highest-security prison in the country. Its nickname? Fittingly, it is known as the "Alcatraz of the Rockies," a "supermax" prison for the most violent of offenders located in Florence, Colorado. The prison was designed solely for solitary confinement and is home to over 400 prisoners. Each of those prisoners spends 23 hours each day alone in their cell, which measures 7 feet by

12 feet. They are given limited contact with the outside world, are given meals through a slit in the door, and must wear handcuffs and leg irons any time they leave their cells.

A former warden of ADX says that, out of all the prisons they've seen, it is by far the most stark and quiet, with everyone separated from one another. Cells have a concrete cell with a foam mattress as a bed, a concrete desk, and a concrete stool. Prisoners are allowed one phone call each month and only three showers a week. They are also limited to how many letters they can write, who they can write to, and how long the letters can be. While ADX was initially built with the intention of being a prison for those who had misbehaved at other prisons, it has more recently become home to many prisoners convicted of crimes related to terrorism.

ADX is home to criminals like Dzhokhar Tsarnaev, one of the Boston Marathon bombers, and Zacarias Moussauoi, one of the men who played a role in plotting the attacks on 9/11. It also houses Thomas Silverstein, a murderer who was moved to the prison after killing a guard at another prison, and Ted Kaczynski, better known as the Unabomber. No criminals have ever escaped ADX, which opened in 1994, and seven prisoners have committed suicide while confined to the prison. Some have argued that the prison falls under the category of "cruel and unusual," but several lawsuits have proven to be unsuccessful.

Reinheitsgebot

Just over 500 years ago, the Duke of Bavaria put a law, Reinheitsgebot, into effect, limiting what ingredients could be used in the beer making process. The law was created in 1516, with the goal of protecting consumers from outrageous prices, keeping brewing companies from using toxic ingredients, and preventing the use of wheat in beer. Before Reinheitsgebot was put into effect, ingredients like wood shavings, rosemary, and soot were used in some beers. At the time, Duke Wilhelm IV wanted to ensure that there was enough wheat to make bread, leading to the banning of wheat as an ingredient. The ban on wheat in beer lasted for years then became a limitation instead of a full-on ban, before it was finally repealed. The law has since been modified, but still restricts what ingredients can be used to make beer in Germany. As replacements for wheat and barley are not allowed under Reinheitsgebot, there is very little, if any, gluten-free beer in the country. The government does, however, allow beer that does not follow the rules of Reinheitsgebot to be imported to the country.

Peanut Butter Diagnosis

Research done in 2013 by a graduate student at the University of Florida found that peanut butter can help diagnose Alzheimer's in the early stage of the disease. Jennifer Stamps was studying under a neurologist when she realized that Alzheimer's patients were not being tested for their sense of smell. As a scientist, she knew that the sense of smell is one of the first things impacted by Alzheimer's and other cognitive problems. The neurologist told her she could organize a test, so long as it would be quick and the materials would be inexpensive. She decided on peanut butter because it is a highly recognizable smell and easy to find on any store shelves.

For the test, Stamps started with one tablespoon of peanut butter, having the patients cover one nostril at a time. She would then move the peanut butter further away from their nostrils, measuring how far the patient was able to detect the smell. The test found that patients who were in the early stages of Alzheimer's had a much more difficult time sensing the odor than those with other variations of dementia. The University of Florida plans to add the test, still using peanut butter, to its rotation of clinical tests performed on patients. While more testing needs to be done in order to fully figure out the relationship between the sense of smell and the development of Alzheimer's, scientists agree that a simple smell test with products like peanut butter is a noninvasive way to detect Alzheimer's earlier.

Salary or Share

In March of 1977, *Star Wars* was an unknown movie, simply a script about outer space with a low budget.

Darth Vader was to be the villain in the movie, but the actor's voice was deemed unfitting for what George Lucas had in mind. He wanted a deeper, more gruff voice. When James Earl Jones was brought in to record voiceover tracks for Darth Vader, he was offered a percentage of the profits for the film, instead of the traditional salary given to actors. Like everyone else, including the studio producing the movie, Jones was skeptical about the movie's potential and thought it would be a flop. He opted to take the salary and earned a mere $7,000 for his voice work, the equivalent of $27,000 today. That was a large amount of money for a struggling actor at the time. *Star Wars* went on to be not only a successful film, but an iconic series. Sir Alec Guinness, who played Obi Wan-Kenobi, accepted the offer of equity, which turned out to be an estimated $95 million.

Distress to Impress

Teens can be quite impressionable, and it is said that many teens will do just about anything to impress their friends. One teenager in Australia took that to the next level and beyond in early 2017. Lee De Paauw was drinking with friends at a hostel in Queensland when he met a girl who captured his interest. He told her that backpackers were more likely than other Australians to be bitten or eaten by crocodiles, which led to a dare. De Pawauw jumped into the Johnstone River, known for being a home to many crocodiles. Upon his entry, he was immediately picked up by a crocodile that measured nearly ten feet long. To break free, he punched the crocodile in the snout and eye until it let go of him. He made it out with treatable injuries to his arm and acknowledged that what he did was reckless. There is a happy ending, however: the girl he was trying to impress agreed to go on a date with him once he made a full recovery.

The Loneliest Whale

A whale that goes by the name of 52 has become known as the loneliest whale in the world. Though it has never been spotted, scientists only know of its existence because its sounds have been picked up through sonar detectors, and 52 got its name because of the frequency of its songs — 52 hertz. Its species is unknown, but the hertz level is one of the highest amongst whales and is not recognized by other whales. Because other whales do not recognize its call, it is never answered, and 52 is left all alone. The whale generally travels alone from the California area to the North Pacific, and it is believed that he has always traveled on his own. Scientists guess that the whale could be a mix between a blue whale and another species, but, without a sighting, they cannot be certain.

Mary Ann Daher has spent a number of years researching 52 and has published papers on the whale and her discoveries. She has received mail from all over the world from people with heartbreaking messages, saying that they can relate to the whale and its loneliness. There have even been songs and stories written about 52. A British rock band released a song called "The Loneliest Whale in the World", while there is a children's book by a German author entitled *52 Hertz Wal.* Scientists and marine enthusiasts alike continue to search for 52, with hopes to better understand the creature and find it a mate.

Roman Athletes

Sports have become an important part of modern culture, and it has been this way for thousands of years. In ancient Rome, hundreds of thousands of people would gather to watch chariot races and naval battles. Drivers for the races were chosen amongst the lower class, and they were given jerseys, helmets, and shin guards, similar to some sports in today's society. The most popular and highly-paid racer in ancient Rome would put even the top athletes today to shame. Gaius Appuleius Diocles played for the Green and White team before making a name for himself as a Red. He spent twenty-four years in the races, earning over 35 million sesterces, the currency of Rome at the time, throughout his chariot racing career. When converted into American dollars with today's value, that would have been a staggering $15 billion Diocles made by the age of 42.

Brain Freeze

How many times have you gone out with friends for ice cream just to hear them yell, "Brain freeze!" after eating too fast?! Brain freeze is actually the common name for sphenopalatine ganglioneuralgia, which is your body's way of telling you to slow down when eating cold foods. Brain freeze occurs because, when you eat or drink something cold, you are changing the temperature in the back of your throat extremely suddenly. This takes place at the internal carotid artery and anterior cerebral artery, both of which are connected to the brain. Brain freeze, though not actually causing pain to your actual brain, becomes the body's way of preventing change from occurring too quickly. There is no official cure for brain freeze, but scientists do advise following common suggestions, like having a lukewarm drink to counter the cold, or putting your tongue against the roof of your mouth for warmth.

Read About Raccoons

When they're not busy rummaging through your trash, raccoons are actually quite complex and fascinating creatures. Raccoons rely on water sources, so they must live within several hundred years of a water source, like a stream or a pond. They are nocturnal for the most part and eat almost any food. As far as prey goes, raccoons often catch smaller creatures like mice, insects, and fish. They can catch fish and turtles with their hands, which have separated pinky and thumb fingers. Due to this dexterity, raccoons are able to take the lids off jars, rip open bags, and undo knots.

The average raccoon lives for between eight and twelve years and weighs between 14 and 25 pounds. They can run up to 17 miles per hour and have whiskers, called vibrissae, on their toes. A raccoon's senses from the front paws alone take up over half of the brain's section that deals with processing senses. These paws are hairless and extremely sensitive, and raccoons use them to wash their food before eating. Raccoons living in and gravitating to urban areas have begun to get up to 20% larger than raccoons that favor woodland areas. Female raccoons are called sows, while male raccoons are known as boars.

Not So Silly

Silly String may be best known as a fun addition to any party, but has also taken on a new role in the United States military. Troops can use Silly String to detect any tripwires, triggering mechanisms, or alarms. The product, also known as party string or aerosol string, can reach up to ten or twelve feet, which allows soldiers to shoot it across an open space before entering. They can tell if there is a tripwire or trap if the string remains hanging in the air instead of falling to the ground.

Many civilians have learned about this newfound use of Silly String and made it their mission to help out. Throughout 2006 and 2007, a woman in New Jersey collected over 80,000 cans of Silly String to send to Iraq. Upon finding out that only a limited number of companies could ship the product, due to the aerosol can it comes in, a company in the woman's local area got in contact with her and agreed to ship the cans to Iraq. Another shipment was sent to Baghdad throughout the waiting period. The packages were labeled with names of individual soldiers, one of whom was the woman's son.

In Postal Service We Trust

One man's faith in the postal service puts the rest of ours to shame. Melvin Milligan won a $46 million lottery jackpot in the state of New Jersey in 2001. Milligan also became the first person in New Jersey lottery history to send the winning ticket in regular mail, instead of opting for insured or certified mail. He had purchased the winning ticket on June 9, 2000, but forgot all about it until the jackpot nearly went unclaimed almost a year later. Upon hearing about the missing ticket on the news, Milligan searched through his junk drawers until he found the ticket he had bought. He took it to a lottery agent, who verified that he had the $46 million ticket. Once the paperwork was filled out, he put the winning ticket in an envelope and sent it in a regular postal service mailbox just two days before the ticket would have expired. His wife worried that the ticket would get lost in the mail, but he didn't think much of it. Lucky for Milligan, the ticket arrived safely at the lottery office, and he was able to claim his winnings, which he took as a $24 million lump sum.

Love from the Beak

Gabi Mann was your average, ordinary eight-year-old from Seattle when she made headlines in 2015 — with one exception. She had befriended the birds in her garden in an extraordinary way. Gabi became known for feeding the birds that came to her yard. Unlike most people, however, the gifts she gave were reciprocated. Gabi has a storage container filled with the "gifts" the crows have brought to her over time. She, with the help of her mother, has catalogued each gift, writing down where in the garden it was left, when it was brought, and what the item was. The birds have brought her everything from Lego pieces, to beads, to paper clips. The container is filled with individually-wrapped pieces of foam, earrings, buttons, and small pins, all from Gabi's flying friends.

When Gabi was just four years old, in 2011, she was known for being clumsy, dropping food on her way out of the car. The birds began to gravitate to her in hopes of foods. When she started attending school, she would share bits of her school lunch with the birds as she walked to the bus stop. The birds began to learn her routine, and would wait for her bus to arrive home each day. With her mom's help, Gabi created a bird feeder in her backyard, leaving everything from peanuts to dog food for the birds to enjoy. The gifts began to appear in her garden from time to time. Some, like a rotten crab claw, went right to the trash, while others, like a rusty screw, have remained amongst Gabi's favorites, cataloged in her container.

Animals in Orbit

For seventy years, animals have been brought—or launched—into space from time to time. The first animals to technically reach space were fruit flies, which were launched in a rocket in 1947. The fruit flies all made it back alive, having traveled nearly 70 miles up in the air. Albert II was the first mammal sent into space. He was a Rhesus monkey sent on a V-2 rocket launched by the United States in 1949. Unfortunately, as the result of a logistical failure, Albert II did not survive.

The Soviet Union sent the first dog to outer space in 1951, but the first dog launched into orbit didn't come until 1957. Laika was a husky that was launched aboard Sputnik 2. A rescue dog that had been found on the streets of Moscow, she died when she ran out of oxygen. Three years later, the Soviet Union tried again. Then sent two dogs, Belka and Strelka, into orbit, along with mice, rats, and a rabbit. This time, all of the animals returned alive and safe.

The first chimpanzee launched into space was named Ham. Trained by NASA, Ham could pull a lever to release bananas to eat and was sent into space in 1961. As of 2015, 32 monkeys have been sent into space. Other animals that have been to space over the years include spiders, cats, frogs, cockroaches, and guinea pigs. The excitement about animals making it to outer space died down once the first man stepped foot on the moon, but animals continue to be sent into space for the sake of research.

Best Thing Since Sliced Bread

"This is the best thing since sliced bread!" How often have we all heard that one? But, the real question is, how long has sliced bread actually been around? Sliced bread was invented by Otto Rohwedder in the late 1920s, with the official patent being filed in 1932. Rohwedder, an inventor in Iowa, created a machine that sliced loaves of bread into individual pieces. At first, bakers did not like the idea. They worried that the bread would become stale too quickly or that the pieces of bread would fall apart in slices. The slices were first held together with pins, in order to ease the worry of those who said the bread would go stale. Once Rodwedder realized what a nuisance the pins were, he began wrapping the sliced loaves in wax paper right after slicing.

Rodwedder had meant for this innovation to be a commercial product, but local bakers still had trouble believing that anyone would care about pre-sliced bread. One company in Chillicothe, Missouri took a chance on the slicing machine. Chillicothe Baking Company sold their own sliced bread, known as "Kleen Maid Sliced Bread". A local newspaper ran a front-page story about the new brand, comparing sliced bread to coffee grounds and pre-sliced bacon. It praised pre-sliced bread as being a time saver. An ad in the newspaper also detailed how to wrap and save the bread for maximum freshness. The success of the bread caught everyone by surprise. Just two years after Chillicothe debuted their brand of sliced bread, Wonder Bread created their own slicing machine and made a name for themselves in the world of sliced bread.

During World War II, the production of sliced bread was banned for two months. The government felt that materials and resources, like the wax paper that had been used to wrap the bread, could be put to better use elsewhere, and that the focus should be on manufacturing products deemed necessary for the war. The public, having gotten used to sliced bread, was not happy about the ban, and it was lifted in March 1943. Sliced bread has remained a staple on store shelves—and in household pantries—ever since.

Rent A Foreigner

Hiring foreigners, generally from western countries like the United States and Canada, has become a common practice for companies in China. These companies believe that having a Caucasian face to put at the front of their business can make the company look more successful and globally important. Over 900,000 foreigners worked in China in 2016, compared to just 10,000 foreigners working in China in the 1980s. One woman from New Jersey found work after she saw a part-time job posting for a foreigner with Chinese language skills. She was chosen for the job, which involved going with the company's director to client dinners. She is paid $145 for each weekly dinner, and her business card lists her title as "Assistant to the Director."

While this new practice has helped many foreigners without the proper skills find work in China, some professionals who have been in the business world for decades are not happy with it. They feel that the foreigners who come in and take over roles for the sake of the company looking diverse are irritating and damaging to the company. Some believe that it is deceitful and dishonest to businesses the companies deal with, and it also brings up the issue of cultural identity. However, the companies have found that hiring Caucasian employees—or employees with Western surnames—has helped with business relations.

Fictitious Name Permit

In California, there is a permit called the Fictitious Name Permit that allows doctors to practice under an assumed or false name. While there are rules, such as the name cannot be deceptive or too similar to another issued name, the only requirement is a $50 fee and a renewal fee every other year. Physicians can be issued as many Fictitious Name Permits as they'd like, so long as they fill out a different application for each one and the name on each permit is different. Generally, these permits are used to add a word or phrase at the end of the doctor's name, such as "Foot and Ankle Treatment" or "Pediatric Specialty". There are no clear bounds as to what is allowed or excluded.

History of the Hawaiian

Though its name may suggest otherwise, Hawaiian pizza was invented in Chatham, Ontario, Canada. Sam Panopoulos was a chef at Satellite Restaurant in the 1960s when he first put pineapples on the pizza. Pizza was fairly new to Canada at the time, with most people only enjoying the food when they visited America. People who visited the restaurant where he worked kept it simple with toppings, mostly limited to bacon, mushrooms, and pepperoni. One day, while using the small pizza oven at the restaurant, Panopoulos simply decided to put some pineapple on top. Customers took to it right away.

Today, an average Hawaiian pizza is a typical cheese pizza with ham and pineapple on top, but Panopoulos maintains that his only innovation was adding pineapple. He says that, in his mind, you can have any variation of pineapple, bacon, mushrooms, or any other topping you'd like. Panopoulos likes to think that his innovation was about more than just creating a new variation of pizza. He believes that it opened the door to combining flavors that never would have otherwise been combined, and inspired other restaurants to try unique creations of their own.

Most Watched-TV Shows

Over the years, there have been hundreds of television shows that have captured millions of viewers. With recording and online streaming options available now, important episodes of TV shows, like season premieres and series finales, don't have the viewers that they used to. Of the top 20 most-watched episodes in television history, based on data taken from Nielsen, they all go back at least fifteen years. The most-watched episode of a TV series in history was "Goodbye, Farewell, and Amen," the series finale of M*A*S*H. The episode had an astonishing 50.15 million viewers. In the number two spot is the series finale of *Cheers*, which had approximately 42 million viewers when it aired in May of 1993.

The third most-watched episode of a TV series was not a season premiere, season finale, or series finale. In fact, it was the fourth episode in the fourth season of *Dallas*. Over 41 million viewers tuned in to see who had shot J.R. Rounding out the top five are the series finale of *Seinfeld*, which drew in 40.5 million viewers, and the series finale of *Roots*, which had around 36 million viewers when it aired in 1977. Surprise episodes on the list? "Say Hello to a Good Buy," season three, episode 15 of *The Cosby Show* ranked sixth, and "Edith's Problem," an episode of *All in the Family* that ranked 20th with 25.2 million viewers. Out of the top 20, *Roots* ruled the list, taking up eight spots.

Starbucks Say What?

Starbucks has over 22,000 locations in over sixty countries, but that's not all that makes the coffee chain stand out. It has been estimated that Starbucks grows by an average of two stores every day, and has been doing so every year for the last 27 years. If you're not sure what type of Frappuccino you'll like at Starbucks, don't worry. There are over 36,000 possibilities for which Frappuccino you can choose, varying by base, syrup, creams, and more. Just at Starbucks alone, consumers use over 4 billion coffee cups each year, and over 20% of those orders are made through the Starbucks app. In 2015, Starbucks set a new record for their sales, reaching $19.2 billion over the course of the year. Throughout the holiday season in 2015, one in every six Americans was gifted a Starbucks gift card.

When Starbucks first emerged on the scene, they only had two sizes: a tall, which was 12 ounces, and a short, which was eight ounces. Today, the sizes range from an 8-ounce short to a 31-ounce trenta. The chain gets its name from the book *Moby Dick*, as Starbuck was the name of the first mate on the ship. The logo was also originally brown, but was changed to green in 1987 because the CEO felt that it was more inviting and affirming. The company plans to open over 3,000 locations in China by 2019. Employees of Starbucks in China get an added bonus unheard of in the United States— the company pays for housing for all full-time employees.

The Fartiste

"The Fartiste" might sound like the name of a character from a cartoon show, but it's actually the name of an off-Broadway musical. The musical is based on a real man, Joseph Pujol, who exhibited such control of his body that he could fart on command and turn his gas into a stage act. Pujol lived during the late 19th century and, though he started off as a baker, he made a name for himself as a professional farter. Charlie Schulman, who wrote "The Fartiste," says that he turned Pujol's story into a show because everyone finds farts funny and he thinks audience members enjoy a good fart joke. One man, Steven Scott, produces all of the farting noises throughout the show with his mouth. In the show, the main character makes a living by putting on shows centered around his farts. Audience members have said that, beyond the obvious humor that comes along with a musical about farts, the show has a positive message about turning an abnormality into a strength. The musical is truly one-of-a-kind, with the main character breaking wind all over the theater, even in the aisles by the audience members.

Man's Best Friend

In 2015, Amazon was voted the most pet-friendly company in America, and it has been named as one of the most dog-friendly companies in the entire world. At the time, around 1,500 employees had dogs registered in the database, all of which had been approved to come to work. The receptionist at the Seattle office keeps a bucket of dog treats on her desk to greet dogs as they come in with their owners in the morning. There are several policies in regard to bringing dogs to work, all of which are basic and understandable. Employees have to get approval from their managers and officemates before bringing their dog into work. They must keep their dog on a leash, except when at their desk, and cannot leave their dog unattended. Dogs must be well-behaved, and they must be registered with the company before coming to work.

A few hundred dogs are on the campus each day, and the tradition dates back to the founding of the company, when the editor-in-chief used to bring Rufus, their Welsh corgi, into work each day. The heads of Amazon have encouraged employees to bring their dogs to work, going so far as to create large courtyards for them to walk their dogs and having dog-sized water fountains for dogs to drink from. Employees say that bringing their canine friends to work helps to relieve stress. The dogs can be seen sitting in their dog beds, laying under their owner's desk, and being walked around the campus.

Hemingway's Hemochromatosis

As far as most of society is concerned, Ernest Hemingway committed suicide in 1961. However, a little-known condition he had was more likely to blame for his death. Hemingway was diagnosed with hemochromatosis, a genetic disease associated with depression, diabetes, liver problems, and high blood pressure, all of which he suffered from, six months before he died. Hemochromatosis is now known as one of the most common hereditary diseases that lead to death in the United States, but not much was known about it then. At the time of Hemingway's poor health, doctors did not know that it was a genetic disease. It causes iron to accumulate at toxic levels, which simultaneously causes organ pain, heart disease, and serious depression. Nowadays, blood tests can easily determine whether or not someone has hemochromatosis, due to the increased levels of iron. Suicide is a common result of untreated hemochromatosis, one that plagued Hemingway's life. The general public did not know about his suffering with the disease until his medical records were discovered in 1991.

History to a Tee

What is now known as the common T-shirt dates back to the Spanish-American War. The United States Navy was issued these shirts, which were short-sleeved and had crewnecks, to wear under their uniform. It soon caught on in the Army, where they decided to make it a standard issue for recruits. T-shirts got their name from their shape, which many felt resembled a "T". They soon became a popular clothing option for farmhands, construction workers, miners, and others who worked outside, as the material was lightweight and made it easier for them in the warm weather. By the early 1900s, T-shirts became more common in everyday society due to the cheap material and the fact that they were easy to clean. Many mothers bought the shirts for their boys to wear while playing or doing chores.

In the 1920s, "T-shirt" was officially entered into Merriam Webster's Dictionary. The first time printed T-shirts were noticed was when *The Wizard of Oz* came out in 1939. Shirts were printed to promote the film, and they became a highly-coveted item. The first printed T-shirt to be photographed was in 1942, when *Life Magazine* featured a man wearing an Air Corps Gunnery School tee on the cover. Mickey Mouse T-shirts followed several years later, as did the popularity of plain white T-shirts after Marlon Brando wore a white tee for his role in *A Streetcar Named Desire*. This became a turning point in the history of the T-shirt, as it was around this time that T-shirts first became acceptable and fashionable as an everyday garment, instead of just as an undershirt or work shirt.

T-shirts took on a new meaning in the late 1960s, when teenagers wore them as a way to express their opinions and pop culture preferences. Shirts throughout the late 1960s and 1970s were designed with political cartoons, band logos, popular icons, and fun phrases. During this time period, T-shirts expanded into more than just the tradition tee. Offerings emerged in a variety of colors, cuts, and styles, ranging from camisoles to crew necks. While putting images and designs on clothing dates back to ancient times, the 1960s saw modern silk screening, heat transferring, and embroidery emerge as the popularity of T-shirts continued to grow.

EPCOT Say What?!

Epcot was opened in Disney in 1982, as an extension of the successful theme park. When it was first opened, its official name was EPCOT Center. The acronym EPCOT stands for "Experimental Prototype Community of Tomorrow", and it was first created by Walt Disney in 1966. He wanted to create a place that was constantly changing, full of new ideas and places. His goal was for EPCOT to be a place for people to live, work, and play, all in one area. After Walt Disney's death, the idea of what Epcot would be shifted, with his brother Roy deciding to focus more on creating a new theme park instead of a community. Epcot has since become an attraction, with international pavilions, rides, and restaurants, but many wonder what it would have been if Walt Disney had been the one overseeing the creation.

Emails Sent: By the Numbers

As of February 2017, there were 3.7 billion users of email services worldwide, and every day 269 billion emails are sent. Broken down, this equates to 2.5 million emails sent every second and trillions of emails sent each year. An estimated 49.7% of all emails are spam messages, and the average person who works in an office receives over 120 emails each day. The email system has been around since 1971, and the highest open rates of email take place on Saturdays. Out of all the companies that send emails to users, Groupon is the company that sends the most emails per user. Only 22.8% of people open political emails, while between 13 and 18% of marketing emails are opened in the United States. The day on which the most email volume is sent is Cyber Monday, the unofficial busiest online shopping day of the year. Only 7.3% of emails are opened on a tablet, while over 55% are opened on a computer. The least effective days to send emails are Wednesday and Friday, and the highest read rate of emails originates in emails with subject lines between 61 and 70 characters.

Six Degrees of Separation

Although celebrities make up a small number of the world population, they still have some interesting connections between them. Karlie Kloss, a famous model, is connected to Donald Trump through her boyfriend. Kloss's boyfriend, Joshua Kushner, is Jared Kushner's younger brother. Jared Kushner is married to Trump's daughter, Ivanka. Randy Jackson and Rebel Wilson are from two very different worlds and generations, but that doesn't make them any less connected. Jackson was a judge on *American Idol* when Adam Lambert was a contestant on the show. Adam Lambert grew up as a friend of Anna Kendrick, who starred in *Pitch Perfect* with Rebel Wilson. How about everyone's favorite purple dinosaur, Barney? Did you know that he's connected to Demi Moore? Barney starred alongside Demi Lovato in several episodes of his show. Demi Lovato was dating Wilmer Valderrama, who co-starred with Ashton Kutcher on *That 70's Show*. Ashton Kutcher was formerly married to Demi Moore.

Franklin for Farts

In addition to Benjamin Franklin's many contributions to United States society, one of his contributions stands out amongst the rest. In 1781, Franklin wrote an essay on the topic of farting. Entitled "To the Royal Academy of Farting" and

"Fart Proudly"—depending on where you read it—the essay makes a case for the importance of creating a medicine to make farts smell better. Franklin said that the smell of farts is offensive, and that the Royal Academy should be putting more resources into creating a drug to reduce the stench. He even argued that this would be one of the biggest accomplishments in medical history and recommended that the medicine be something that could be mixed with sauces or other foods. Despite writing the essay to the Royal Academy, Franklin instead sent it to some of his friends, including a chemist and philosopher. While the essay was written in a tongue-in-cheek nature, Franklin called for not only the reduction in negative smell from farts but something that would make them smell as nice as perfume.

Real Names of Celebrities

Many of your favorite celebrities weren't born with the names you have come to know them by. For a variety of reasons, they have taken on stage names, middle names as first names, and different last names. Katy Perry was born Katy Hudson, but she changed her name because she felt it sounded too similar to actress Kate Hudson. Demi Moore was born Demetria Guynes, but shortened her name. Natalie Wood was born Natalia Nikolaevna Zakharenko to parents who had immigrated from Russia. In order to have a name that she felt would fit better in Hollywood, she shortened her first name and changed her last name. Tina Fey's real name is Elizabeth Stamatina Fey. She shortened her middle name and adopted it as her stage name.

Nobody knows who Caryn Johnson is, but Whoopi Goldberg is a household name. Goldberg chose Whoopi as her first name due to her farting abilities, and she ended up with Goldberg because her mom thought that having a Jewish-sounding last name would help with her career. Hulk Hogan was born Terry Jean Bollette, but clearly that name doesn't sound quite as intimidating as Hulk. Frederick Austerlitz took on a more Americanized version of his name, and became who we now know as Fred Astaire. Bruno Mars? He was born Peter Gene Hernandez. Doesn't have quite the same ring to it, huh?

Before Marilyn Monroe was a sex symbol in Hollywood, she was little Norma Jean Mortensen, who got picked on in school. Natalie Portman simplified her name by switching out the last name she was born with, Herschlag, to her grandmother's maiden name. Dezi Arnas's name is catchy and easy to say, but his birth name wasn't quite so simple. He was born Desiderio Albert Arnaz y De Acha III. Eileen Regina Edwards became a country icon in the late 1990s and early 2000s as Shania Twain. Shania is quite a bit catchier than Eileen, while Twain is the last name of the man her mother married when she was young.

Forming and Breaking a Habit

While it is a common myth that it only takes 21 days to form a habit, a more recent study done at University College London found that the average amount of time it takes for a habit to stay is 66 days. The study, which followed the habits of nearly 100 people over the course of a twelve-week period, found that the amount of time it takes varies by individual. In this particular study, it ranged from just 18 days to 254 days. The timeline for breaking a habit is thought to be similar, as breaking a habit is virtually the same thing as creating a new habit without that component in your life. Psychologists agree that there is no exact time frame for how long it takes to break a habit, as it depends on the person's individual circumstances, level of motivation, and personality type.

Some habits can be broken instantly, if an extreme incident happens that impacts the individual. Nearly choking on cigarette smoke could cause someone to give up smoking right away, while someone would likely stop sending text messages while driving if they nearly crash their car. Psychologists and researchers say that the best way to break a habit is to form a new habit that replaces the old one. Most people are unable to stick to a new habit or break an old one because they quit after several weeks of no results. This idea of taking only 21 days to form a habit comes from a popular book in the 1960s, with no research to back up the claims. Your brain must have time to adapt to a new pattern of response, whether the habit you're trying to start is going to the gym in the morning, cutting out a cup of coffee each day, or keeping from biting your nails.

Goat Skin Laws

In a time when modern technology rules all, the United Kingdom keeps some of their traditions old-fashioned. For over one thousand years, the United Kingdom has printed all of their laws on vellum, which is made from the skin of calves or goats. When the House of Lords made the decision in 2016 to end the printing on vellum due to budget cuts, the Cabinet Office stepped in and decided to provide the money in order for the transcribing of the laws to continue. The first known vellum document of the United Kingdom parliament dates back to 1497. Some argue that the British should switch over to a digital archive, while others like that the tradition has remained for all these years.

Vellum, from the same root as the word "veal", is made from the skin of calves, soaked in a wash, then scraped to remove any animal fat. It is then stretched onto a frame and scraped for added evenness. Once the skin is completely dry, it can be used for writing. Digital archivists worry that something will happen to the vellum and that all records of the laws will be lost, while calligraphers argue that technological outlets can change and that digital data could be impossible to read down the line. They compare it to floppy disks, which were once the common way of sharing information when computers first became popular. Vellum is known for staying in good condition for hundreds of years. One prime example is the Magna Carta, which was written on vellum and still exists 800 years after its signing.

Raise the Right

The modern tradition of raising the right hand while taking an oath dates back to London in the 17th century. Unlike today's society, there were no written criminal records for judges to know a person's criminal history, and there were no set punishments for certain crimes. Thus, the judges at the time were able to choose from any punishment of their choosing, ranging from a simple pardon, to a death sentence. Sometimes, they opted for brandings, which entailed placing a branding iron on the defendant's body. They could be branded with "F" if they were a felon, "M" for murderer, and other initials to indicate their crimes. Before the branding of hands became common, thieves in London were branded on the face, in the cheek area, but it was deemed to be too damaging to the convicts' futures. If these criminals passed through the courts again, they were asked to raise their right hand, in order to allow the judge to see if they had any brandings. This would indicate whether or not they had committed any crimes in the past. The raising of the right hand has been a tradition in courtrooms ever since.

Antoine's Restaurant

Antoine's is a restaurant in the French Quarter of New Orleans, known as a family restaurant that counts Oysters Rockefeller and Baked Alaska amongst its signature dishes. Antoine's also has another feat to its name: it is the oldest continuously-run family restaurant in America. The restaurant dates back to 1840, when Antoine Alciatore, a 27-year-old from France, decided to open up a small restaurant and hostel with his wife. Alciatore died 30 years later due to health problems and his wife soon took over. When their son, Jules, was old enough, he took over the restaurant and came up with many of the signature dishes that are still served today. Jules married into a wealthy family, who helped him convert the small restaurant into an 800-person restaurant with 14 dining rooms.

In the 1920s, Jules' son took over Antoine's Restaurant, and ran the restaurant for over fifty years. Upon his death, the restaurant was passed on to his nephews, then to one of his nephews' sons, then to the other nephew's son, and finally to his cousin, Rick Blount. Rick Blount's daughter, Casie, has been groomed to take over the business when he is no longer able to. The restaurant has a staff of nearly 160 people, many of them related to the original owner through blood and marriage. Each member of the staff spent several years in a training program before becoming official members of the staff team. They have seen such notable patrons as Presidents Kennedy and Nixon, Joan Rivers, and Pope John Paul II. The restaurant has thrived for decades, through two world wars, Prohibition, and numerous hurricanes. When Hurricane Katrina hit, the restaurant suffered only minimal damage, and it took just four months for the building to be fixed up to its previous appearance. Over the years, Antoine's Restaurant has been owned by five generations of Antoine Alciatore's family, and the sixth generation is already preparing to take over.

DON'T FORGET YOUR FREE BOOKS

MORE BOOKS BY BILL O'NEILL

I hope you enjoyed this book and learned something new. Please feel free to check out some of my previous books on **Amazon**.

Sources:

http://www.hyperthymesia.org

http://www.businessinsider.com/guess-which-day-set-the-record-for-most-flowers-sold-in-the-us-2015-6

http://philadelphiaencyclopedia.org/archive/rocky/

http://www.imdb.com/title/tt0075148/trivia

http://historynewsnetwork.org/article/1109

http://www.digitaljournal.com/article/341910

https://www.unclaimedbaggage.com/

http://www.huffingtonpost.com/2014/08/08/graham-cracker-history-sexual-urges_n_5629961.html

http://www.npr.org/2014/12/31/373982308/hockeys-doc-emrick-and-his-153-verbs

http://thebiglead.com/2014/02/21/doc-emrick-used-153-words-to-describe-puck-movement-in-the-usa-canada-game/

http://www.unibo.it/en/university/who-we-are/our-history

https://www.cnet.com/news/youtube-started-as-an-online-dating-site/

http://travel.cnn.com/explorations/life/15-worlds-weirdest-museums-268795/

http://www.huffingtonpost.com/travel-leisure/americas-strangest-museum_b_4269790.html

http://www.huffingtonpost.com/2014/01/13/divorce-lawsuit_n_4590440.html

http://www.pbs.org/wgbh/nova/nature/dogs-sense-of-smell.html

http://www.naa.gov.au/collection/fact-sheets/fs144.aspx

http://www.cbc.ca/news/business/mcdonalds-kale-calorie-questions-1.3423938?cmp=rss

http://www.dailymail.co.uk/news/article-2348644/The-highest-calorie-menu-items-Americas-10-fast-food-chains-revealed--surprised.html

http://ew.com/article/2015/07/14/bobs-burgers-eugene-mirman-parking-ticket/

https://www.usatoday.com/story/life/entertainthis/2014/05/15/alex-trebeks-daily-breakfast-snickers-and-a-diet-pepsi/77287630/

http://www.nytimes.com/1982/05/25/us/ohio-candidate-tells-of-paying-for-prostitute.html

http://www.nydailynews.com/sports/football/smelling-salts-nfl-head-injuries-article-1.2675345

https://www.moviefone.com/2012/04/02/titanic-movie-mistakes-james-cameron/

https://www.scientificamerican.com/article/looking-at-the-sun-can-trigger-a-sneeze/

http://historydetectives.nyhistory.org/2014/08/blast-past-tiny-incubator-babies-coney-island-attraction/

http://www.fodors.com/news/photos/worlds-10-coolest-ice-hotels

http://www.nydailynews.com/news/world/99-year-old-italian-man-divorces-96-year-old-wife-finding-secret-love-letters-1940s-article-1.998455

http://www.cnn.com/2010/LIVING/07/03/mf.baby.naming.laws/index.html

http://nation.time.com/2013/08/12/from-messiah-to-hitler-what-you-can-and-cannot-name-your-child/

https://comicvine.gamespot.com/zeitgeist/4005-15531/

http://metro.co.uk/2015/09/18/japanese-women-can-now-hire-good-looking-men-to-wipe-away-their-tears-5397164

http://listverse.com/2011/07/13/10-hard-to-translate-english-words/

https://www.theguardian.com/notesandqueries/query/0,,-187912,00.html

http://blog.ted.com/40-idioms-that-cant-be-translated-literally/

https://www.washingtonpost.com/national/religion/bhutan-takes-a-second-look-at-phallus-worship/2014/03/03/1e9ff838-a310-11e3-b865-38b254d92063_story.html?utm_term=.b5bdb3e73752

http://www.metro.us/local/study-shows-subway-air-samples-include-human-skin/tmWmeh---f3ziRPgXKo9U

http://www.independent.co.uk/news/science/aboriginal-australian-searching-toilet-stumbles-49000-evidence-earliest-human-settlement-a7394731.html

https://www.boston.com/uncategorized/noprimarytagmatch/2012/05/24/harvard-alumni-association-apologizes-for-listing-unabomber-ted-kaczynskis-awards-his-life-sentences-for-terror-campaign

https://www.casino.org/news/lavish-living-for-the-richest-tribe-owning-indian-casinos-in-america

http://trove.nla.gov.au/newspaper/article/102017012

http://abcnews.go.com/blogs/headlines/2012/09/second-mona-lisa-unveiled-for-first-time-in-40-years/

http://www.traveller.com.au/pilots-flying-high-on-a-first-class-menu-ghs3b7

https://www.theguardian.com/music/tomserviceblog/2013/dec/09/symphony-guide-haydn-102-miracle

http://m.sfgate.com/news/article/Hawaii-s-hot-rocks-blamed-by-tourists-for-bad-2920041.php

https://www.encyclopedia-titanica.org/titanic-survivor/bertha-mayne.html

http://newsfeed.time.com/2010/12/10/bea-arthur-tough-chick-her-secret-past-as-a-marine/

http://www.delish.com/food/news/a37312/the-gingerbread-man-personality-test/

https://mobile.nytimes.com/2004/12/04/arts/television/star-of-tennis-but-not-tv-mcenroe-loses-his-talk-show.html

https://www.mi5.gov.uk/agent-garbo

http://www.hottubworks.com/blog/spa-hot-tub-or-jacuzzi-whats-the-difference/

https://www.findagrave.com/cgi-bin/fg.cgi?page=gr&GRid=49460775

http://untappedcities.com/2014/11/13/daily-what-nyc-bus-driver-steals-own-bus-drives-to-florida-in-1947/

http://www.nydailynews.com/news/crime/oklahoma-new-york-battle-life-killer-thomas-grasso-article-1.475703

http://mentalfloss.com/article/30659/founder-mothers-day-later-fought-have-it-abolished

http://www.washingtonpost.com/wp-dyn/content/article/2007/08/17/AR2007081702365.html

http://www.nytimes.com/1994/07/07/nyregion/corruption-uniform-dowd-case-officer-flaunted-corruption-his-superiors-ignored.html

http://www.nytimes.com/2013/09/05/nyregion/the-six-figure-price-tag-for-selling-a-two-dollar-hot-dog.html

http://www.popularmechanics.com/technology/design/g446/4339347/

http://wonderopolis.org/wonder/who-invented-cotton-candy/

https://www.bostonglobe.com/metro/2015/04/25/the-alcatraz-rockies/a0BWrZjRpmQatMsfm8FUOL/story.html

http://www.huffingtonpost.com/2013/04/30/twins-born-87-days-apart-ireland-guiness-record_n_3186135.html

http://www.aivaliotis.com/greece/anthem.shtml

http://www.businessinsider.com/12-crazy-facts-you-probably-didnt-know-about-starbucks-2016-2

http://www.huffingtonpost.com/2011/11/16/the-fartiste-musical_n_1082637.html

http://www.seattledogspot.com/dog-friendly-businesses/amazon-dog-friendly-seattles-dog-friendliest-company/

http://www.webmd.com/add-adhd/childhood-adhd/food-dye-adhd

http://celticcurse.org/hemingways-death-and-hemochromatosis-awareness/

http://www.teefetch.com/history-of-the-t-shirt/

https://www.amazon.com/gp/product/1941500269/

http://www.inquisitr.com/1752042/why-did-benjamin-franklin-write-an-essay-about-farting-and-why-his-idea-might-come-true/

http://www.mensjournal.com/expert-advice/12-things-everyone-should-know-about-vaginas-20150114/penis-captivus

https://www.youtube.com/watch?v=er7d1-Mis4o

http://www.businessinsider.com/american-children-see-253-mcdonalds-ads-every-year-2013-11

http://www.sciencealert.com/here-s-how-long-it-takes-to-break-a-habit-according-to-science

http://blogs.reuters.com/photographers-blog/2011/05/05/monowi-nebraska-population-1/

http://www.ourgeorgiahistory.com/ogh/Atlanta's_Winecoff_Hotel

http://www.smithsonianmag.com/science-nature/why-do-mosquitoes-bite-some-people-more-than-others-10255934/?page=1

http://onemileatatime.boardingarea.com/2017/02/12/eva-air-hello-kitty-pictures/

http://www.herald.ie/news/clown-funeral-service-will-let-your-loved-one-go-with-a-smile-27899932.html

https://talesofthecocktail.com/culture/porco-lounge-creates-world-record-shattering-daiquiri

http://www.herald.ie/news/clown-funeral-service-will-let-your-loved-one-go-with-a-smile-27899932.html

http://www.businessinsider.com/why-matchcom-owns-princeton-review-2015-10

http://public.oed.com/history-of-the-oed/

https://www.census.gov/newsroom/releases/archives/mobility_of_the_population/cb11-193.html

http://www.criminaljusticeusa.com/blog/2011/10-famous-ex-cons-who-turned-it-around/

http://www.expatica.com/es/insider-views/Top-10-obscure-driving-laws-in-Spain_596547.html

http://www.slate.com/articles/life/gentleman_scholar/2014/02/is_pointing_rude_yes_but_etiquette_gives_gentlemen_other_options_for_gesturing.html

http://www.popularmechanics.com/technology/design/g446/4339347/

http://www.hollywoodreporter.com/news/verizon-phases-can-you-hear-178679

http://blog.justbats.com/why-is-a-baseball-game-nine-innings

http://www.huffingtonpost.com/2013/04/30/twins-born-87-days-apart-ireland-guiness-record_n_3186135.html

http://www.mensjournal.com/expert-advice/12-things-everyone-should-know-about-vaginas-20150114/penis-captivus

http://articles.latimes.com/2001/sep/09/local/me-43719

http://wonderopolis.org/wonder/who-invented-cotton-candy/

http://www.contactmusic.com/beatles/news/the-beatles-helped-break-down-racial-segregation-by-refusing-to-perform_5387579

https://usatoday30.usatoday.com/life/lifestyle/2004-08-11-baby-carrot_x.htm

http://health.howstuffworks.com/skin-care/information/anatomy/shed-skin-cells.htm

http://nypost.com/1999/07/22/buckingham-booze-hounds-queen-bites-aide-who-got-corgis-drunk/

http://www.avclub.com/article/seventeen-minutes-of-lost-footage-from-i2001-a-spa-49219

http://www.skydiving.com/news/2017/skydiving/accidents/female-skydiving-enthusiast-survives-plummeting-14500-feet-onto-fire-ant-mound/#.WShOLE7OZ0Q.reddit

http://wonderopolis.org/wonder/how-powerful-is-stomach-acid

http://www.bbc.com/news/uk-england-39434504

https://www.vice.com/en_us/article/alan-smithee-is-officially-the-worst-hollywood-director-of-all-time-456

http://thehigherlearning.com/2014/04/26/the-unbelievable-story-of-the-japanese-man-who-survived-both-atomic-bombs/

https://www.marketplace.org/2011/11/16/life/freakonomics-radio/your-thanksgiving-turkey-probably-product-artificial-insemination

https://www.universetoday.com/38599/astronaut-helmet/

http://www.bbc.com/future/story/20170525-the-people-who-speak-in-whistles

http://www.atlasobscura.com/places/sourtoe-cocktail

http://www.alanarnette.com/blog/2016/12/18/how-much-does-it-cost-to-climb-mount-everest/

http://mentalfloss.com/article/77099/10-big-facts-about-giant-ground-sloths

http://entertainment.time.com/2007/10/29/top-25-horror-movies/slide/bambi-1942-2/

https://www.mnn.com/earth-matters/climate-weather/blogs/how-hurricanes-are-named-and-why

http://ajournalofmusicalthings.com/science-shows-singing-heavy-metal-makes-big-baby/

http://www.telegraph.co.uk/news/worldnews/europe/spain/8174180/Spanish-woman-claims-ownership-of-the-sun.html

http://www.cleveland.com/globalvillage/index.ssf/2013/07/euclid_square_mall_now_home_to.html

http://www.clevescene.com/scene-and-heard/archives/2017/05/04/empty-euclid-square-mall-may-soon-officially-bite-the-dust-as-developer-eyes-location/

http://mentalfloss.com/article/70783/5-writers-who-really-hated-shakespeare

https://vanwinkles.com/what-s-the-longest-amount-of-time-someone-has-stayed-awake

http://www.mnn.com/earth-matters/wilderness-resources/stories/what-can-28000-rubber-duckies-lost-at-sea-teach-us-about

http://mentalfloss.com/uk/law/31712/why-is-there-confetti-in-so-many-taser-guns

http://www.npr.org/templates/story/story.php?storyId=7639868

https://mobile.nytimes.com/2017/03/01/magazine/sand-mining-india-how-to-steal-a-river.html?_r=0&referer=

http://www.glamour.com/story/find-lost-wedding-ring

https://www.vice.com/en_us/article/over-the-edge-134-v16n9

http://ultimateclassicrock.com/the-doors-banned-from-the-ed-sullivan-show-september-17-1967/#photogallery-1=28

http://russiasgreatwar.org/media/military/women_soldiers.shtml

http://deadspin.com/36-cheap-american-beers-ranked-638820035

https://mobile.nytimes.com/2014/09/21/magazine/how-gary-harts-downfall-forever-changed-american-politics.html?referer=

https://www.logaster.com/blog/dominos-logo/

https://www.theguardian.com/football/2017/mar/06/francis-kone-player-could-have-died-togo-czech-republic

http://www.npr.org/sections/parallels/2015/10/21/450235327/londons-cabbies-say-the-knowledge-is-better-than-uber-and-a-gps

http://www.rollingstone.com/music/news/metallica-play-a-dome-in-antarctica-20131209

http://www.atlasobscura.com/articles/how-first-ladies-on-opposing-sides-of-the-civil-war-forged-an-unlikely-bond

https://www.colormatters.com/color-and-marketing/color-branding-legal-rights

http://www.telegraph.co.uk/news/worldnews/australiaan

dthepacific/pitcairnislands/11418280/Why-will-nobody-move-to-Pitcairn-the-Pacific-island-with-free-land.html

https://www.theguardian.com/news/datablog/2014/jul/31/germany-the-worlds-capital-of-penis-enlargment-country

http://www.history.com/news/scientists-reveal-inside-story-of-ancient-egyptian-animal-mummies

https://www.businessinsider.com.au/china-has-some-very-strange-criteria-for-selecting-its-flawless-female-astronauts-2012-3?r=US&IR=T

http://www.okhistory.org/publications/enc/entry.php?entry=TE026

http://www.npr.org/sections/thetwo-way/2016/11/18/502551138/dying-teenager-in-u-k-wins-right-to-be-cryogenically-frozen

http://ultimateclassicrock.com/bono-things/

https://www.theatlantic.com/business/archive/2012/04/americas-dumbest-tax-loophole-the-florida-rent-a-cow-scam/255874/

http://universalstudios.wikia.com/wiki/True_Lies

http://mentalfloss.com/article/57718/15-fun-facts-about-true-lies

https://www.vice.com/en_us/article/having-a-ball-or-two-at-the-montana-testicle-festival-999

https://www.theatlantic.com/technology/archive/2016/08/can-twitter-fit-inside-the-library-of-congress/494339/

https://twitter.com/librarycongress/status/12169442690

http://www.thepunctuationguide.com/em-dash.html

https://www.historicmysteries.com/what-happened-to-bobby-dunbar/

https://blog.hrc.utexas.edu/2015/07/30/throwback-thursday-contents-of-a-country-leicester-hemingways-republic-of-new-atlantis/

https://www.oneweirdglobe.com/destination-worlds-coon-dog-cemetery-alabama/

https://www.theguardian.com/science/2016/jan/20/flat-earth-believers-youtube-videos-conspiracy-theorists

https://www.usatoday.com/story/news/nation-now/2013/12/09/mort-crim-ron-burgundy-anchorman-will-ferrell/3889937/

http://www.hollywoodreporter.com/heat-vision/pirates-caribbean-stars-share-stories-set-1008242

https://www.etiquettescholar.com/dining_etiquette/table_manners/resting_utensils_etiquette.html

http://m.huffpost.com/us/entry/1579277

http://www.popularmechanics.com/technology/a21457/the-gif-is-dead-long-live-the-gif/

http://ew.com/article/2016/04/29/human-centipede-2-high-school/

http://nypost.com/2011/06/26/brazen-bulger-toured-alcatraz-while-on-the-lam/

https://www.thecarguys.net/indy_500_racing_facts.pdf

https://vinepair.com/articles/the-bizarre-history-behind-fika/

http://www.npr.org/2011/03/26/134379296/the-secret-bunker-congress-never-used

http://www.huffingtonpost.com/2013/07/18/wyoming-has-only-2-escalators_n_3616861.html?m=false

http://time.com/4686280/subway-chicken-fast-food-filler/

http://abcnews.go.com/US/September_11/saving-kareena-sept-11-attacks-stopped-infants-transplant/story?id=14437024

https://www.theverge.com/2017/2/15/14622646/mulan-niki-caro-female-director-disney

http://archive.boston.com/business/articles/2011/08/07/the_inside_story_of_keurigs_rise_to_a_billion_dollar_coffee_empire/

http://nypost.com/2013/12/24/how-scrooges-of-park-avenue-stiff-doormen/

http://www.businessinsider.com/turkmenistans-dictator-just-built-a-huge-golden-statue-of-himself-riding-a-horse-2015-5

http://q13fox.com/2014/12/29/united-airlines-sues-22-year-old-who-found-way-to-get-cheaper-plane-tickets/

https://www.usatoday.com/story/news/nation/2013/03/11/water-americas-favorite-drink/1978959/

http://m.huffpost.com/us/entry/1895505

http://www.historytoday.com/peter-clements/silent-cal

http://www.jta.org/2016/09/14/news-opinion/israel-middle-east/worlds-oldest-man-a-holocaust-survivor-in-israel-to-celebrate-bar-mitzvah-100-years-late

https://www.thelocal.it/20161216/snack-selling-schoolboy-given-suspension-and-scholarships

http://www.carscoops.com/2013/09/brazilian-man-plan-to-bury-his-bentley.html?m=1

http://www.ed.ac.uk/medicine-vet-medicine/about/history/women/james-barry

http://www.washingtonpost.com/wp-dyn/content/article/2008/07/11/AR2008071103281_pf.html

http://content.time.com/time/specials/packages/article/0,28804,1891335_1891333_1891322,00.html

https://academic.oup.com/jhmas/article-abstract/47/1/49/770426/Scurvy-and-chronic-Diarrhea-in-Civil-War-Troops

http://www.theindyexperience.com/indy_dvds/dvd_legend.php

http://www.telegraph.co.uk/news/uknews/law-and-order/6023749/Sex-offender-jailed-after-burglars-find-child-porn-on-his-laptop-and-turn-him-in.html

http://www.atlasobscura.com/articles/how-a-tribe-is-fighting-off-loggers-with-a-drone-they-built-watching-youtube

https://blogs.wsj.com/speakeasy/2009/11/07/bert-ernie-are-they-or-arent-they-kurt-andersen-expounds/

https://www.theguardian.com/technology/2016/jun/22/mark-zuckerberg-tape-webcam-microphone-facebook

http://nypost.com/2014/03/02/hotel-hermit-got-17m-to-make-way-for-15-central-park-west/

https://www.ncbi.nlm.nih.gov/pmc/articles/PMC1121900/

http://www.cnn.com/2016/01/25/us/dog-runs-half-marathon/

http://abcnews.go.com/Business/CEOProfiles/story?id=4573076&page=1

https://www.ucf.edu/pegasus/harris-rosen/

http://www.latimes.com/local/lanow/la-me-ln-pepsi-fire--jackson-20130509-story.html

http://mentalfloss.com/article/64881/good-will-hunting-scripts-hidden-secret

http://www.today.com/food/making-chicken-sandwich-scratch-took-six-months-1-500-t45091

http://money.cnn.com/2016/03/16/technology/homemade-invisalign/

http://www.themeparkinsider.com/flume/201312/3819/

http://www.snopes.com/college/homework/unsolvable.asp

http://abcnews.go.com/US/whitey-bulger-life-sentences-boston-crime-wave/story?id=20886205

http://www.goodhumor.com/article

http://abcnews.go.com/Entertainment/story?id=7926226

http://m.huffpost.com/uk/entry/4744161

http://woodtv.com/2016/02/15/battle-creek-reaches-settlement-with-4-female-officers/

http://www.telegraph.co.uk/science/2016/03/12/30-minute-ice-packs-could-be-key-to-burning-away-body-fat-say-sc/

http://mentalfloss.com/article/66502/15-sweet-facts-about-step-brothers

http://www.history.com/news/10-words-and-phrases-popularized-by-presidents

http://articles.latimes.com/2009/jul/07/opinion/oe-standage7

http://www.bbc.com/news/world-asia-china-36220142

http://www.npr.org/2007/10/25/15629096/identical-strangers-explore-nature-vs-nurture

http://www.npr.org/2008/02/19/18950467/hercules-and-hemings-presidents-slave-chefs

http://www.history.com/news/history-lists/eight-times-queen-victoria-survived-attempted-assassinations?cmpid=FACEBOOK_FBPAGE__20170530&linkId=38173632

http://www.bbc.com/news/entertainment-arts-22145306

https://www.theguardian.com/world/2008/oct/09/zimbabwe

http://edition.cnn.com/2009/WORLD/africa/02/02/zimbabwe.dollars/

https://www.newsday.co.zw/2014/01/30/zimbabwe-use-chinese-currency/

https://mobile.nytimes.com/2006/01/29/science/japanese-scientists-identify-ear-wax-gene.html?referer=

https://medlineplus.gov/ency/article/000373.htm

http://m.chron.com/news/houston-texas/article/Authorities-ignore-fugitive-holed-up-on-Texas-1693380.php#item-39786

http://money.howstuffworks.com/us-coins-no-numerical-values.htm

https://www.wired.com/2010/12/news-update-farm-animals-get-80-of-antibiotics-sold-in-us/

http://articles.latimes.com/1987-08-29/business/fi-1391_1_brotman-medical-center

https://thinkprogress.org/all-the-special-snowflakes-aaf1a922f37b

https://mobile.nytimes.com/2016/09/14/world/what-in-the-world/australia-magpie-season.html?referer=https://www.bing.com/search?q=swooping+season&qs=n&form=QBLH&sp=-1&pq=swooping+season&sc=5-15&sk=&cvid=E74D7EFF7068466A8F48F887455EA3A0&referer=

http://www.today.com/health/need-mom-new-service-lets-you-hire-one-advice-home-t53766

http://www.montana.edu/everest/facts/morefacts/ff06.htm

http://www.atlasobscura.com/articles/strong-me-the-rise-and-fall-of-the-toothpick-capital-of-the-world

http://www.smithsonianmag.com/travel/tattoos-were-illegal-new-york-city-exhibition-180962232/

http://articles.latimes.com/1998/mar/29/news/mn-33836

http://www.newsweek.com/2014/09/05/north-korea-owes-sweden-eu300m-1000-volvos-stole-40-years-ago-still-using-267043.html

http://www.bbc.com/news/world-us-canada-20777866

https://www.theguardian.com/notesandqueries/query/0,5753,-19637,00.html

https://www.thestar.com/news/canada/2017/04/28/three-men-sentenced-for-18-million-quebec-maple-syrup-heist.html

http://www.bbc.com/news/world-europe-40110169

https://www.theguardian.com/notesandqueries/query/0,5753,-2036,00.html

http://historydetectives.nyhistory.org/2012/07/blast-from-the-past-newsboy-strike-of-1899/

https://www.sciencedaily.com/releases/2003/03/030328073214.htm

http://www.telegraph.co.uk/news/uknews/1561604/Key-that-could-have-saved-the-Titanic.html

http://www.medindia.net/facts/

https://postalmuseum.si.edu/parcelpost100/p4.html

https://mobile.nytimes.com/blogs/cityroom/2013/06/04/long-ago-a-pilot-landed-on-an-uptown-street-thats-where-the-bar-was/?referer=

http://www.nbcnews.com/news/world/auschwitz-survivor-gena-turgel-walked-out-gas-chamber-alive-n293496

https://www.theatlantic.com/business/archive/2012/01/jack-daniels-secret-the-history-of-the-worlds-most-famous-whiskey/250966/

http://mentalfloss.com/article/67806/early-trains-were-thought-make-womens-uteruses-fly-out

http://www.thedailybeast.com/dont-laugh-at-natalie-portman-and-jonathan-safran-foers-intense-letters

http://www.bbc.com/news/magazine-36882799

http://www.news.com.au/travel/travel-ideas/weird-and-wacky/inside-the-festival-of-the-steel-phallus-in-kawasaki-japan/news-story/1e70c04df0268d3184c7baa68dc2c919

https://www.beach.com/islands/its-illegal-to-visit-this-island-in-the-indian-ocean-and-heres-why/

http://www.smithsonianmag.com/history/spoonful-sugar-helps-radioactive-oatmeal-go-down-180962424/

https://news.vanderbilt.edu/2016/12/21/allergists-say-alpha-gal-red-meat-allergy-better-understood-as-numbers-continue-to-increase/amp/

https://la.curbed.com/2013/5/23/10241002/13-facts-about-las-most-annoying-icon-the-lapd-helicopter

http://m.radioaustralia.net.au/international/2011-12-13/413710

https://www.theguardian.com/environment/2016/jul/13/us-food-waste-ugly-fruit-vegetables-perfect?utm_source=esp&utm_medium=Email&utm_campaign=GU+Today+USA+-+morning+briefing+2016&utm_term=181590&subid=17882768&CMP=ema_a-morning-briefing_b-morning-briefing_c-US_d-1

http://www.oddee.com/item_98018.aspx

http://www.cbsnews.com/news/once-conjoined-twins-celebrate-10-years-of-separate-lives/

https://sports.vice.com/en_us/article/the-plot-to-kill-the-slam-dunk

http://www.foodsafetymagazine.com/magazine-archive1/aprilmay-2003/why-consumers-take-risks-with-food-safety/

http://home.howstuffworks.com/lenox.htm

https://consumerist.com/2015/06/29/report-finds-100-walmart-com-products-labeled-made-in-u-s-a-that-were-made-elsewhere/

http://time.com/12597/the-ukraine-or-ukraine/

http://time.com/money/4166577/guinness-record-credit-card-holder/

https://www.organicfacts.net/health-benefits/beverage/whiskey.html

http://militaryhistorynow.com/2012/07/10/a-shitty-little-war-peru-fights-spain-over-animal-turds/

http://www.kidsdiscover.com/quick-reads/angels-glow-the-bacterium-that-saved-civil-war-soldiers/

http://www.cnn.com/2017/03/20/world/china-toilet-paper-thieves-face-recognition-trnd/index.html

http://modernfarmer.com/2014/02/chicken-feathers/

http://gothamist.com/2010/06/17/world_trade_centers_sky-high_subway.php

http://www.nbcnews.com/id/38960380/ns/health-mental_health/t/trapped-still-sane-survivors-disaster-speak-out/

http://civilwarsaga.com/conjoined-twin-eng-bunker-drafted-during-the-civil-war/

https://crimewatchdaily.com/2016/03/07/baby-killing-nurse-approaches-expected-release-from-prison/

http://abcnews.go.com/Entertainment/rapper-dep-burden-lifted-confessing-murder/story?id=20322228

http://www.espn.com/nhl/story/_/id/19452424/2017-stanley-cup-real-story-playoff-beards

https://mobile.nytimes.com/2016/07/03/us/canada-alaska-hyder-stewart-british-columbia.html

http://articles.sun-sentinel.com/1993-07-03/features/9301220063_1_dinosaur-million-years-jurassic-park

http://www.clevedonhypnotherapy.co.uk/brief-history-of-hypnosis/

http://www.yesterland.com/wizard.html

https://journalistsresource.org/studies/economics/personal
-finance/research-review-lotteries-demographics

http://www.saintmarksphiladelphia.org/sermons/2009/10/
11/pew-rent.html

https://m.thevintagenews.com/2017/05/11/candy-desk-
one-desk-in-the-us-senate-chamber-is-always-filled-with-
candy/

http://www.nytimes.com/1994/07/07/nyregion/corruption-
uniform-dowd-case-officer-flaunted-corruption-his-
superiors-ignored.html

http://www.aivaliotis.com/greece/anthem.shtml

https://www.bostonglobe.com/metro/2015/04/25/the-
alcatraz-rockies/a0BWrZjRpmQatMsfm8FUOL/story.html

http://www.businessinsider.com/12-crazy-facts-you-
probably-didnt-know-about-starbucks-2016-2

http://www.huffingtonpost.com/2011/11/16/the-fartiste-
musical_n_1082637.html

http://www.seattledogspot.com/dog-friendly-
businesses/amazon-dog-friendly-seattles-dog-friendliest-
company/

http://www.webmd.com/add-adhd/childhood-adhd/food-
dye-adhd

http://celticcurse.org/hemingways-death-and-
hemochromatosis-awareness/

http://www.teefetch.com/history-of-the-t-shirt/

https://www.amazon.com/gp/product/1941500269/

http://www.inquisitr.com/1752042/why-did-benjamin-franklin-write-an-essay-about-farting-and-why-his-idea-might-come-true/

https://www.youtube.com/watch?v=er7d1-Mis4o

http://www.businessinsider.com/american-children-see-253-mcdonalds-ads-every-year-2013-11

http://www.sciencealert.com/here-s-how-long-it-takes-to-break-a-habit-according-to-science

http://www.bbc.com/news/world-europe-36110288

http://www.medicalnewstoday.com/articles/267236.php

http://www.celebritynetworth.com/articles/entertainment-articles/1977-james-earl-jones-demanded-salary-front-instead-points-star-wars-chose-poorly/

http://www.telegraph.co.uk/news/2017/03/21/australian-teen-bitten-crocodilelooking-forward-date-british/

http://www.odditycentral.com/animals/the-heartbreaking-story-of-the-worlds-loneliest-whale.html

http://www.laphamsquarterly.org/roundtable/greatest-all-time

https://www.sciencedaily.com/releases/2013/05/130522095335.htm

http://www.animalfactsencyclopedia.com/Raccoon-facts.html

http://www.nydailynews.com/news/80-000-cans-silly-string-collected-troops-iraq-article-1.230724

http://abcnews.go.com/US/story?id=93095&page=1

http://www.bbc.com/news/magazine-31604026

http://www.nationalgeographic.com.au/space/animals-in-space.aspx

http://mentalfloss.com/article/49168/brief-history-sliced-bread

http://m.scmp.com/news/china/society/article/2096341/white-people-wanted-peek-chinas-booming-rent-foreigner-industry

http://www.mbc.ca.gov/Applicants/Fictitious_Name/Fictitious_Name_FAQ.aspx

http://www.foodnetwork.ca/shows/great-canadian-cookbook/blog/the-history-of-hawaiian-pizza/

http://www.businessinsider.com/most-watched-episodes-2016-9/#20-all-in-the-family--ediths-problem-1

http://www.businessinsider.com/12-crazy-facts-you-probably-didnt-know-about-starbucks-2016-2

http://www.huffingtonpost.com/2011/11/16/the-fartiste-musical_n_1082637.html

http://www.seattledogspot.com/dog-friendly-businesses/amazon-dog-friendly-seattles-dog-friendliest-company/

http://www.teefetch.com/history-of-the-t-shirt/

https://disneyparksmomspanel.disney.go.com/question/letters-epcot-stand-263735/

https://www.amazon.com/gp/product/1941500269/

https://www.lifewire.com/how-many-emails-are-sent-every-day-1171210 http://people.com/celebrity/six-degrees-of-separation-celebrity-edition/karlie-kloss-donald-trump-4-degrees

http://www.inquisitr.com/1752042/why-did-benjamin-franklin-write-an-essay-about-farting-and-why-his-idea-might-come-true/

https://www.vox.com/2015/1/13/7533665/benjamin-frankling-farting

http://www.sciencealert.com/here-s-how-long-it-takes-to-break-a-habit-according-to-science

http://thoughtcatalog.com/nico-lang/2013/08/55-celebrities-whose-real-names-will-surprise-you/

http://www.bbc.com/news/magazine-35569281

https://nwsidebar.wsba.org/2013/10/21/raise-right-hand-court/

http://www.latimes.com/nation/la-na-antoines-20130509-dto-htmlstory.html